Also by Jeffrey G. Allen, J.D., C.P.C.
How to Turn an Interview into a Job

FINDING THE RIGHT JOB AT MIDLIFE

by
Jeffrey G. Allen, J.D., C.P.C.
and Jess Gorkin

Simon and Schuster
New York

To all those silent superstars
Who don't believe they can have it;
Those almost achievers
Who haven't reached it; and
Those present performers
Who want even more.
May these pages live
Through your successful midlives.

SIMON AND SCHUSTER and colophon are registered
trademarks of Simon & Schuster, Inc.
Designed by Irving Perkins Associates
Manufactured in the United States of America

1 2 3 4 5 6 7 8 9 10

Library of Congress Cataloging in Publication Data

Allen, Jeffrey, 1943–
Finding the right job at midlife.

Bibliography: p.
Includes index.
1. Job hunting.   2. Middle aged men—Employment.
3. Middle aged women—Employment.   I. Gorkin, Jess.
II. Title.
HF5382.7.A45   1985   650.1'4'0240564   85-2313
ISBN: 0-671-53058-5
ISBN: 0-671-55548-0 Pbk.

Contents

be at the mercy of another employer again.

are particularly attractive security
for midlifers. Here, you'll learn
how to present the idea and prepare the agreement so it will be
accepted. It's your job insurance
policy, so *go for it!*

Introduction

Your success in re-entering the job market or changing jobs after the age of 40, really comes down to just three things:

1. Developing the right attitude about your abilities;
2. Organizing an effective job campaign; and
3. Overcoming the myths in our society about midlife employees.

After over two decades of assisting people of different ages and stages, and making two major career changes myself, I am convinced that *anyone* can find or create a job in midlife. It's just a matter of bringing the wisdom of age within yourself to bear upon a youth-oriented culture.

As you start to apply the techniques and use the information that follows, you will find that opportunities exist you never dreamed possible. You will also find that self-esteem and productivity are ageless.

This is more than a book about finding a job. It is a book about finding *yourself*. After all, the world has been changing—types of jobs, age-related discrimination laws, longer lives. No wonder it's left so many behind. But that's what makes it so challenging. You haven't been growing older, you've been growing smarter!

The best example is my co-author, Jess Gorkin, who began a new career as editor of *50 Plus* magazine after 30 years as editor-in-chief of *Parade* magazine, and whose wisdom has informed this book.

About a year ago, I met with someone in our law office who had become a multimillionaire in his thirties, and lost virtually everything as a result of the last recession. The purpose of our visit was to reorganize his business. Unlike many who were in a similar position, he had all of the enthusiasm of a decade before, when he first started. After our meeting I commented on this, and his answer was incisive: "I know exactly how I made my first million and a lot more after that. I also know exactly how I lost it all." Less than six months later, he made his second first million. Knowing where he went wrong was at least as important as knowing what he did right.

Even before you were old enough to answer, you probably were asked: "What do you want to be when you grow up?" Aside from your name and age, almost every adult you met seemed preoccupied with your answer. Your first encounter with formal education may have been the beginning of your "career guidance." Testing, subject emphasis, recreational activity, class standing, and social pressure all structure and program our careers to adulthood. But where do you go from here? Time to set aside the preconceptions, rationalizations, and excuses. It may not be easy, but it *will* be exciting!

By now, you've learned that there are winners and losers in every field, and that success has more to do with savvy, knowledge, and well-timed effort than with chance or luck. Therefore, my mission is to give you as much practical information as possible regarding your options, and to help you select among them.

Your life experience will be your most valuable resource, and I'll be showing you how to mine it, turn it into a tangible asset, and market it properly.

In view of the history of unemployment among midlife women, it is tempting to use feminine terms throughout the book. However, in the interest of readability, the masculine gender is predominant. While most of the information applies to either sex, special advice to middle-age women re-entering the job market has been included.

CHAPTER 1

New Jobs for Older People: What, Where and Now!

If you've been thinking that your middle-age status is a barrier to employment, you might be interested in a few official statistics: In 1975 there were 19.3 million men and 12 million women employed over the age of 45. In 1981, the number rose to 22.1 million men and 13.1 million women.[1] This represents a combined increase of 3.9 *million* people in just six years! Today, the figure is estimated at about *double* that number, or almost 8 million *more* midlifers in the workforce during the past decade. They are in all walks of life and in thousands of different jobs.

During this time, the birth rate has declined, while the average life span has increased by one year for every year since Social Security began. Women have re-entered the job market after raising families. These are major trends.

Fully 75 percent of all new jobs in America are in service-oriented, non-manufacturing pursuits. Economists call this "de-industrialization," and you'll become very familiar with that word. More people are engaged in the distribution of products than actually produce them. These service jobs are expected to double in the next decade. Consulting is emerging as one of the most popular

11

ways to market services. We'll be helping this trend along in Chapter 7. How much more perfect for midlifers could our economy be?

Here is a list of some of the occupations included:

Accountants and Auditors
Actors and Actresses
Actuaries
Architects
Assemblers
Attorneys*
Bank Officers, Managers
  and Tellers
Bartenders
Broadcast Technicians
Buyers
Cashiers
Chefs and Cooks
Computer Systems
  Analysts, Programmers
  and Operators
Computer Technicians
Corrections Officers
Cosmetologists
Dental Assistants and
  Hygienists
Dentists*
Designers
Dietitians
Electricians
Electronics Technicians
Engineers
Guards
Health Service
  Administrators

Insurance Brokers, Agents,
  Underwriters and
  Claims Adjusters
Laboratory Technicians
Legal Assistants
Nurses and Nursing
  Aides
Occupational Therapists
Office Machine
  Technicians
Opticians
Optometrists*
Physical Therapists
Physicians*
Psychologists*
Real Estate Brokers and
  Agents
Receptionists
Recreation Instructors
Reporters
Retail Salespeople
Secretaries
Securities Brokers and
  Agents
Social Workers
Surveyors
Teachers
Teachers' Aides
Travel Agents
Writers and Editors

* Usually requires advanced formal education.

105 million jobs. And you only need to find one.

See anything you like? It can be yours, and I'll show you how as you turn the pages. In fact, you can pick more than one job. I'll even show you how to do *that!*

This list has been developed by reviewing several surveys and is intended to demonstrate only two things: None of the jobs require excessive physical strength and almost none require advanced formal education. Those that offer certification (accountants, actuaries, architects, etc.), invariably accept experience in lieu of education and recognize part-time education through correspondence, evening and summer programs, "crash courses," or simply by passage of equivalency examinations.

If you are entering the job market after a long absence, the best thing to do is jump right into *skills training*. An entry-level job is the optimum way, since you'll "earn while you learn." Classified advertisements, public and private placement offices, and "cold-calling" businesses that have jobs in the field—*any* jobs—are the places to start. If you can afford it, volunteer time in exchange for training can also be valuable. The only classes to consider are those that teach specific, marketable *skills* or have a "work component." Sitting somewhere listening to abstract theory may be fine for youngsters, but if you're not careful, midlife will pass you by. Employers want *skills*.

If you are changing jobs, try to resist the temptation to change careers abruptly. Midlifers too often attribute career stalls to their careers rather than their jobs. Can you really afford to start at the bottom again? Why not just bring that invaluable experience to bear somewhere else?

In conducting outplacement programs, I discovered that there is over 50 percent "job comparability" or similarity between all occupations, so far as the day-to-day work is concerned. However, if you "go for what you know," it can be much higher. For almost every formerly employed midlifer, there is a prospector who has abandoned an active gold mine. There are thousands of younger trainees seeking employment in every field for each job that is occupied. As the sign says: "Top dollar paid for old gold."

My strategy was no different from others who used each job as a step to the next: Placement counselor to personnel manager, to placement attorney, to author in the employment field. Gradually growing, each success building on the one before. You can do it too. It's a fact of midlife:

> Your value to a new employer increases directly with the necessary skills you bring to the job.

An important exercise is to write down the jobs related to your present one ("job family"), then those that require similar skills ("cross-over jobs"). While the first list may look like a combination of Scrabble and Trivial Pursuit, reworking it a few times will start your mind creatively expanding the options. Although you may already be familiar with the job family, you can discover many cross-over jobs by reading the *Dictionary of Occupational Titles,* annually published by the United States Department of Labor. It contains the names and brief descriptions of thousands of jobs, and is available at your public library reference desk.

There is a great difference between skills that are *actually* transferable and those that can be *marketed* as transferable. The employer doesn't know unless you emphasize the transferable skills. Therefore, it is often helpful to work *backward,* taking the job description and plugging in your applicable experience to the resume and dialogue. If you are like most midlifers, before long you will be astounded at how closely your skills are aligned with the job you are seeking. This is because your wealth of life experience just needs focusing. And marketing.

Present and future jobs must be filled, and midlifers are a natural. Employers who haven't learned that experienced, mature employees are usually better employees, will find this out by necessity through not being able to hire anyone else.

Dramatically improved health care has been a predominant factor that will continue to assure a robust work force from our major segment of the population. To employers, this means that absenteeism and work-related errors are no longer reasons to reject midlife candidates. Once they are hired, group health, workers' compensation, and related rates don't rise.

In 1967, the federal Age Discrimination in Employment Act[2] made it official: Age discrimination in jobs is against the law. This is binding upon private enterprises with 20 or more employees, all federal, state and local governments, and labor unions. It even extends to the activities of employment agencies, executive recruiters, and others in the placement process. While federal law designates 40–70 as the age sector for protection (with no upper limit for federal employees), many states have expanded this to include *any* age discrimination whatsoever. As a midlifer, you should also be aware that discrimination on the basis of medical condition,[3] physical handicap,[4] or sex[5] is also prohibited.

Our offices specialize in the laws relating to employment, and during the past decade, we have noticed a dramatic reduction in the number of midlife discrimination incidents. Undoubtedly, legislation and the well-publicized cases interpreting it have contributed to an awareness of the problem, but necessity and technology will eventually eliminate it. Your middle-age status shouldn't become a legal issue if you follow the principles we will be discussing.

A public awareness is emerging that middle age actually exists and really isn't cause for an inferiority complex after all. Most important, midlife is being recognized as the most productive, contributive, enjoyable place from womb to tomb.

The jobs are here *now!*

CHAPTER 2

An Age-Old Problem: the Younger Generation

One of the first psychological signs of midlife is noticing the apparently high energy level of people in their twenties and thirties. Regardless of whether it's a new employee on the job, a salesperson at the store, or simply observing the activities of a younger family member, the natural inclination is to feel very, very tired. Perhaps you've even wondered how you could ever compete against these attractive, healthy human specimens. This is often called an inferiority complex, or "low self-esteem." It is also an optical illusion. Let's examine how the world of work really favors more mature individuals:

As automation replaces manual labor in almost every area of work, the importance of physical strength is diminishing. I could cite thousands of examples, but this is so obvious that you need only look around to see that no mass-produced items are manufactured by human hands any longer.

The Industrial Revolution has merged into the computer age, and between now and the end of the twentieth century, it is predicted that repetitive jobs will practically disappear. For us, this means your score on the nineteenth century carnival "strength-o-meter" just doesn't matter anymore.

If you observe youthful workers, you will notice that, although they move about rapidly, they don't necessarily accomplish more than their older counterparts. It's subtle, but when you're at the early stages of learning any job, there's a lot of wasted motion.

Several years ago, a client of ours developed an extremely successful placement service with an unusual approach. Soon, imitators copied the marketing technique and even the internal operations. Since proprietary rights were involved, and a number of the imitators were former employees, you might suspect major litigation arose. However, she didn't consider this a threat to her empire. When I asked her why, she replied,

> They can imitate all they like. They can copy everything I've developed, and they won't succeed. What matters isn't my successes, it's my *failures!* These people will never learn all of the lessons my mistakes taught me.

This placement service continues to double its revenue each year. Virtually every "look-alike" looks a lot different. Most have left the placement field entirely.

This is the subtlety of experience. I see it every day in the practice of law. We all obtained our licenses the same way, we all use big words, we're all wearing vests. Ask any judge: That's just the beginning.

You've probably forgotten the incredible amount of pressure on young adults to achieve. I graduated from a program in night law school at the age of 30, supporting two families with full-time jobs as a placement counselor and personnel manager. Two years later, I was eating lunch at a restaurant and saw a supervisor with my former employer. After exchanging greetings she asked, "How did you manage to become a lawyer with all of your responsibilities?" I don't know where the words came from, but I replied, "What is surprising is not that I *did it,* but that I *lived through it!*" If you think about your own achievements in your twenties and thirties, you will probably have the same "past shock." It's an unsettling time when young adults are still taking required courses in the school of hard knocks. They may be more energetic, but they're not more efficient.

Our society has glorified youth, but you don't have to internalize this as a barrier to finding a rewarding occupation. Your physical strength doesn't matter; your experience and the perspective of a more organized life style do. Soon, age will become nothing more than an excuse to become unemployed.

In the bestseller, *Looking Out for Number One,* Robert Ringer captured the essence of how to bridge from experience to the job (or anything else) you want:

> Paying one's dues isn't necessarily analogous to age or number of years of experience. Some people are ready at 20, others aren't ready at 70. Nobody knows what you've gone through to prepare yourself; by the same token, you should never be presumptuous enough to resent someone else's seemingly quick ascent to the top. You don't know what the other guy went through to get there.[6]

This is an insidious problem among midlifers, and therefore it will be necessary to pull as much of the age bias out of your subconscious as possible. Only then will you be able to recognize its fallacy.

Just prepare a list like this:

IDEAL JOB LIST		
Job Title	**PERCENT OF ACTIVITY** Mental	Physical
1.		
2.		
3.		
4.		
5.		
6.		
7.		
8.		
9.		
10.		
11.		
12.		

Choose jobs that you would like to do. They will tend to be those that are far more dependent upon brains rather than brawn. Why? Just another minor midlife change in your outlook.

You can easily over-engineer your career planning with questionnaires, charts, graphs, schedules, logs and diaries. The minutiae and regimentation of these can interfere with your creativity, cause you to procrastinate, and make you feel guilty about not filling in the blanks as prescribed.

At best, they are boring and time consuming. That is why I'll be keeping the forms simple and fun.

Youth isn't really "wasted on the young." It's the only way to make it to midlife!

Now, it's just a matter of learning to *go for what you know.*

CHAPTER 3

You've Come a Long Way, Maybe!

After living for a while, we have a tendency to forget that employers are not just looking for experience. They are looking for *selective* experience. The same is true of customers. Therefore, it makes no difference whether you will be working for someone else or joining the 6 million people who started their own businesses during the last decade. The key is to translate general life experience into specifically marketable attributes:

> Experience is not what you've done,
> It's what you do with what you've done.

One of our clients in the placement field has a full-length mirror in the reception room of her office, with a sign that reads: "WOULD YOU HIRE THIS PERSON?" That mirror reflects that you are selling yourself in a buyer's market, and as much as possible will be reviewed.

Midlife is also an excellent time to consider a career change. Since you are looking for another position anyway, it's the same nickel. (Now, *that's* a midlife expression!)

You may have to offset salary for opportunity, but statistically, you're in the best position to do so now.

Regardless of whether you will be stepping in, over or up, that full-length mirror will be staring you in the face. Let's check you out:

Start with your employment history, and *write down* every job you've held. My inventory started with a job scooping ice cream and, looking back, I *must* have been the original "one minute manager." Since you are exploring all of the options, be as accurate as possible. It doesn't require more than one sentence for each job function. You can even include volunteer jobs.

A helpful guide looks like this, using one page for each job, and numbering them consecutively starting with the first:

JOB NO. _____
_____ to _____
year   year
Name of Employer or "Self"
Name of Job
most significant responsibility
next most significant responsibility
next most significant responsibility
next most significant responsibility
next most significant responsibility

We're not checking your memory for dates, your preferences in job duties, or how much you earned. We're just inventorying your experience. Since you are largely the product of this experience, each of these former activities affects your present attitudes, goals, and marketability to others. Most people don't realize how much "job comparability" actually exists between such apparently different positions as president of the PTA and director of administration. Most jobs are only structured activities for the purpose of efficiency. It all started back when the cavemen first discovered the merits of a division of labor.

The inventory is a self-analysis exercise, but many people find it is also valuable to use when reviewing their qualifications with employers. Perhaps you worked in a grocery store as a teenager because your family needed the financial assistance. This demonstrates an early sense of responsibility. Perhaps you did so to earn enough money to buy a car. This shows your willingness to work toward a goal. The fixed hours of work meant you had to prioritize your time and schedule effectively. Is this really important now that you are a midlifer? It was to you then, and your basic personality hasn't changed. Your past is definitely the key to your future. Of course, the amount of responsibility tends to increase with each job number.

Next, you should review your achievements. As with jobs, the earlier ones will seem inconsequential. In fact, if you're like most people, even your *latest* ones will. How little we look in that mirror! Now is the time, so I recommend use of a simple list like the one shown. I've filled in the first few items as a guide.

You'll be reminding yourself of those spelling bee trophies, scouting merit badges, and sports awards that are stored in the attic of your mind for rare occasions like this. If it helps, go through your dresser drawer or scrapbook. How important it all was then! *Now* do you see how absurd it is to worry about competing with younger adults?

DATE(S)	ACHIEVEMENT	REQUIRED ATTRIBUTES
1. *6/56*	*Vice President of 11th Grade*	*Leadership ability, popularity and integrity.*
2. *9/57*	*High School Football Team*	*Coordination, ability to work with others and competitiveness.*
3. *6/58– 9/58*	*Theater Usher*	*Neatness, punctuality, courtesy and responsibility.*
4.		
5.		
6.		

As you move toward the higher numbers on the list, working your way through college, job promotions, or community service awards may come to mind.

The first lists you make may be somewhat disjointed and out of chronological order. However, as you rework them, you will be sensitizing yourself to the kind of job you want, and how to obtain it.

Now, you're ready to convert the information into usable form. Write down your answers to the following questions:

1. What are your primary attributes?
2. What are your primary liabilities?
3. Which jobs did you like most?

4. Which achievements are you most proud of?
5. Do you like working in a large or small organization?
6. Do you like working for someone else or being your own boss?
7. Do you like supervising others?
8. Do you like to work with people or with things?
9. Do you like to be paid on a salary or a commission basis?
10. Do you like to travel?

Don't worry about the length of your answers or what anyone else thinks. This is *your* midlife!

For the last exercise, prepare another sheet like the one on page 23, and give it the final job number. Complete it for your ideal job. Be realistic, but be creative, since most jobs—particularly ones that midlifers occupy—require the exercise of independent judgment. Imagine that you have been offered a job where you can write your own ticket. Consider your attributes, *and* your liabilities (although by now, it's not easy). Do you really need an advanced college degree, or will your experience be sufficient? Most important, tailor the job to what you would really like to do. You deserve it!

If you include an agreeable boss, office decor, or the number of paid holidays, you will be defeating your purpose, so don't digress. Really concentrate on your goal: the job you are determined to get.

It is easy to read through this chapter without doing the exercises—too easy, in fact. The real value comes from meticulously researching your own life to prove your case to *yourself* for the job you want.

> Life is stored backward,
> but can be steered frontward.

And if you're going to sell yourself, it is imperative to understand that:

It's impossible to motivate an employer
above the level of your own enthusiasm.

Following the exercises carefully may not seem important until it is over. But they give a powerful push to the
midlife career stall. The positive change in your attitude
and ability to direct your efforts will be dramatic.

You've come a long way, *definitely!*

CHAPTER 4

Jobkeeping: Playing the Game

Most midlifers were brought up believing that "working hard," "doing a good job," or "keeping their nose clean" would ensure job security. Unfortunately, this overlooks the most important, pervasive, and volatile aspect of every group formed since the dawn of civilization—*politics!*

Politics is nothing more than a manifestation of the struggle for power, often resulting in midlife casualties. Understand the rules, and you will stay in the game until the techniques in the book get you major-league offers.

If you are an employee with seniority, a key position, a large staff, or ownership in the company, you are probably a "power broker" yourself. But most people are not, especially those considering a career change.

Informal chains of command or "power bases" radiate from these power brokers, often reaching every corner of the building. Where do you begin?

You begin in the most obvious place:

The boss may not always be right, but he's always the boss.

Your supervisor is in power, or at least in control, and is therefore essential to your jobkeeping strategy. At this point, it would be a mistake to jeopardize what you have for what you want, so let's keep you employed until you're ready to make a move.

When faced with a complaint from an employee, the personnel professional is trained to ask, "Have you spoken to your supervisor about it?" The answer is invariably something like "Are you kidding? Everybody *knows* you can't talk to him!" Ask the supervisor, and he'll not even be aware a problem exists. I estimate that this communication blockage accounts for over half the "latent hostility" most midlife employees haul around.

"Your boss is human." Obviously, you think. Still, many older employees really don't believe it. You can tell by the way they act. They fear their bosses like gods and scorn them like lower forms of life at the same time. The numbers, forms, and rules just serve to dehumanize the relationship even more.

Unfortunately, stereotyping your boss and venting your feelings of persecution and frustration won't keep you on the job one extra day. The problem is the *interaction* between your boss and you.

Don't expect your boss to take the initiative. American industry has already tried "forced communication" (yes, that's what it's called) with formal performance reviews. I administered these for almost a decade. Let's look at them more closely:

The procedure generally consists of the employee listing his accomplishments and "goals." The supervisor does so independently, and a formal meeting is arranged. The supervisor, even if well-intentioned, knows that all of the documents will be placed in the permanent personnel folder. He also knows that his boss and his boss's boss will be "reviewing" the "performance." The nervous subordinate also knows about "The Book" and is rendered totally defenseless.

Show me a company that has a periodic review system, and I'll show you a company that can't even get its *super-*

visors to comply! Organized confrontation, preying on the insecurity of middle-age employees.

You've probably been involved in this game, and either felt or buried some pretty negative feelings about your boss and yourself. But your job security depends on both of you, and the solution is not going to be found in mechanical review systems.

The single most important way to hold on to your job is to make yourself indispensable to your boss. This requires a whole new way of perceiving him, and a willingness to take a clear view of your own objectives. Promise yourself that you are not going to let yourself react negatively or passively to your boss's role. Recognize him as somebody who may well be anxious or insecure in his own job—and remember, the more difficult managers behave, the more likely they are insecure. Your supervisor has his own boss to contend with, and undoubtedly has his own problems. If you can find ways to help solve them, he'll perceive you in a favorable way, and may even begin to trust you with information or assignments that he would never even have considered delegating before.

One of the first steps you can take to subtly indicate this new attitude is to behave in a cheerful and positive manner.

Dale Carnegie's classic work, *How to Win Friends and Influence People*, has good advice to help you bury the hatchet *and* the axe:

> The employment manager of a large department store told me he would rather hire a salesgirl who hadn't finished grade school, if she had a lovely smile, than to hire a doctor of philosophy with a sober face.
>
> The chairman of the board of directors of one of the largest companies in the United States told me that, according to his observations, a man rarely succeeds at anything unless he has fun doing it. This industrial leader doesn't put much faith in the old adage that hard work alone is the

magic key that will unlock the door to our desires. "I have known men," he said, "who succeeded because they had a rip-roaring time conducting their business. Later I saw those men begin to work at the job. It grew dull. They lost all joy in it, and they failed."

You must have a good time meeting people if you expect them to have a good time meeting you.[7]

The Dale Carnegie courses have been assisting those in midlife since 1912, and have won tens of millions of friends and have influenced tens of millions of people all over the world. They instruct students to smile at someone every hour of the day for a week and then report the results to the class. You don't have to be a student to obtain the benefits. Almost every expert on success agrees with this principle, and in fact studies have shown that smiling really does make you feel better. I am not aware of any statistical study on the subject but have assisted hundreds of supervisors in deciding who to terminate among thousands of choices under many varied conditions, and a clear pattern emerges. Mature people who are enjoyable are the ones you try a little harder to retain, even if it means finding them another job. A genuine, sincere, pleasant smile on the face of a subordinate who looks you in the eye is worth as much as a willingness to work overtime! *Cheerful spirits give everyone a lift,* so check your frown lines.

If you feel you could use some improvement in this area, the way to use the technique is to decide you're really going to make an effort to be more pleasant, and then develop a game plan for your "smile" campaign. For example, you might even write down one phrase to say to your boss for each day of the week, like:

Monday: How was your weekend? (Listen attentively.) This looks like another busy week already!

Tuesday:	I'm really looking forward to working on the *(name of project)* job.
Wednesday:	What do you think about improving the *(name of project)* job? I'd like to try it.
Thursday:	Is there anything I can do to help you? I've been really busy lately, and haven't had a chance to ask.
Friday:	I'll be taking home the *(name of project)* to work on over the weekend. I want to get a head start for next week.

Be casual but sincere, and don't overdo it. At first, you may feel a little self-conscious, but soon, smiling and speaking affirmatively will be as natural as cashing your paycheck.

After several weeks of this "human relations" exercise, increased communications and friendliness with your boss will follow. You'll gradually sense the change in his response as well. However, you should resist the temptation to inquire about your future with the company. As my father, a law professor, taught me on the eve of my first trial:

You don't ask the question unless you know the answer.

Let's look at why:

a. If he says your job is *secure,* you'll be sorry you asked. If he wasn't already thinking about it, you've made it easier to discuss again. You've also called attention to your *own* doubts about your midlife ability.
b. If he says your job is *not secure,* you probably won't hear anything else after that. Regardless of the reason for the negative response, your smile will be less natural. "Suggestions for improvement" can be translated into additional midlife concern when you know your job is on the line.

Don't telegraph your fears to your boss when it's a no-win proposition.

Now that you're communicating, the most effective way to stay interesting to most bosses is by subscribing to at least one monthly magazine in your occupation. The latest "buzz words," state-of-the-art ideas, and ways to improve your job are likely to be discussed somewhere in every issue. Even the articles you *don't* like are often good topics of conversation. If you don't know the name of the magazine, stop by your local library, and ask the reference librarian to look it up for you in *Readers' Guide to Periodicals, Ayer Directory of Publications,* or some other source. Virtually every field has at least one publication (*Advertising Age, Engineering Times, Mortuary Management,* etc.). If the library carries it, you can read it there or tear out the subscription card and receive it at your home regularly. It is easy to lose touch with what is happening in any field, and this is a super job-enhancing device. In the future, you might even want to submit a comment or article. This *really* boosts your jobkeeping and job finding credentials. However, just receiving and reading the publication every month or so may make an important difference to your job security.

Trade associations are better for "networking" to find jobs (as we'll see in Chapter 9) than to learn about them, but they are a primary source to expand your professional acquaintances.

Job-related subscriptions and association expenses are tax-deductible, incidentally, so if you're not reimbursed, declare them yourself.

As you work on establishing a strong relationship with your boss, you'll also want to find opportunities to mention your accomplishments. It may not make sense to be persuaded by salespeople talking about their merchandise, but we all are. Your boss is no exception. You can advocate yourself without being too obvious by "spontaneous" remarks. For instance, you might say, "Didn't the *(name of project)* we worked on turn out well? It made us all look good!"

Whenever appropriate, write a brief memorandum to your boss, summarizing the results of an exceptional job, meeting, or public relations activity in which you participated. Interesting pictures (trade shows, etc.) might also be included. If you mention it in advance, he might be delighted if you send it to other power brokers. It should start something like, "I am pleased to report the results of the *(name of program)* program."

If you work for a large company, your name and picture in the employee newsletter is another jobkeeper. Contact the editor and offer to provide departmental material on a continuing basis. The pause on the other end of the line will be the editor picking himself up off the floor. Contributing requires little more than a loaded instant camera and almost no writing skill. In fact, submission of many articles is done by telephone. I used to be an editor of these, but my title should have been "Ghostwriter." I was ecstatic just to be able to say another employee was on the "staff." I really fought to keep them around. *My* job security depended on it!

Even if you can't always eliminate the negative, you can accentuate the positive. In fact, you *must!* The person who said "It doesn't matter who gets the credit as long as the job gets done" probably just received credit for something.

Other ways to keep your job are:

1. Stress the importance of "doing a good job," and don't feel embarrassed about occasionally using company slogans (if they exist);
2. Determine and extol the real virtues of the company, (nobody likes insincerity);
3. Suggest ways to improve operations (by increasing efficiency, reducing costs, developing new products, etc.); and

4. Never take it upon yourself to criticize the management or direction of the company. Somebody's going to be hurt, and it's probably going to be you.

Almost all supervisors complain about how difficult it is to find employees who "really care." Loyalty is highly prized. No manager wants to feel that a person reporting to him will undermine his efforts, whether intentionally or through indifference. In the years I spent as a personnel manager, I am convinced that my most valuable role was "keeper of the company line." Although my bosses never knew it, sometimes it was my *only* role.

The next power broker that you should work on is your boss's boss. This is best done through your boss, never around him. Following the chain of command is much safer than going around the "firing authority." In addition, "company people" revere the organization chart and standard operating procedures. There is a saying in the corporate world that "going around your boss is heresy." It is a classic trap for midlifers, since they are often older than their supervisors.

Even if your boss's boss asks you to perform a little industrial espionage on your boss for him, you'll lose trust and respect by consenting. It is imperative that you gracefully decline with words like "I'm sorry, but I report to *(your boss's name)*. I hope you understand, but it would be inappropriate." No long-winded explanations; just leave it at that. Don't agonize over it—you won't be asked again. You just increased your job security. The midlife jobkeeper's credo is:

Those who stay watch what they say, and watch to whom they say it.

Opportunities to impress your boss's boss arise frequently; a day your boss is out, an after-hours visit, answering a telephone when your boss is busy, etc. You'll be utilizing the rule:

Smile, it will make people wonder what you're up to.

You will also find that the increased rapport with your boss will make him less defensive. He'll want to show you off because it makes him look like a good manager.

There are very few jobs that you can't keep if you really want to—and know the right techniques. But there is always the possibility that the worst will happen even to the best employee. That is a subject we will explore next.

CHAPTER 5

The Layoff Survival Kit

The statutory and case law surrounding employment discrimination is extremely technical and sometimes inconsistent. The burden of proof is difficult, and prosecuting claims through government agencies or the court system is often a frustrating, expensive, degrading ordeal.

Since enactment of the Civil Rights Act of 1964, I have watched the equal employment opportunity laws evolve from the perspective of an employee, personnel manager, affirmative action officer, and attorney. Simply stated, the *threat* of filing a "charge of discrimination" is far more useful than the *act* of doing so. Even the newly emerging field of "wrongful termination" is just a cane, and for some midlifers, a crutch. You probably don't need it and the animosity that even threatening it can engender makes it a last resort—a last-ditch effort to save a job you can't save by the positive, potent techniques in this book.

With that understanding, there are two parts to using the layoff survival kit, so you stay on the job as long as possible: Symptoms and Treatment.

SYMPTOMS

There are ten basic ways that employers telegraph invol-
untary terminations before they occur. If you notice more
than one, it's probably time to open the kit. A few tests to
verify your diagnosis are also included.

1. Changes in Attitude and Dialogue

When a company is ailing, its personality changes, just like
an individual's does. If you know how it normally "feels"
and "talks," you won't need a thermometer to tell if it has
"fling fever."

A change in attitude by management is usually evi-
denced by closed doors, a preoccupation with the status of
pending matters, and irritability. The typical supervisor
wants to be left alone because he's probably a midlifer
thinking about his future. However, he also has to justify
his present job. This accounts for the erratic "keystone
cop" routine: out he comes from his office asking about
how you're doing on the same project he asked about five
minutes ago. Unless you recognize the symptoms, you'll
be living the old saying:

> If you can keep your head when everyone around you is
> losing theirs, you don't understand the situation.

Corporate dialogue also changes. Conversations and
memoranda from management change from words like
"develop," "train," and "analyze" to "curtail," "reduce,"
and "expedite." You can see that they're scurrying about,
getting their affairs in order . . . often one of the first signs
of a terminal illness.

Whatever they have is catching. Better get organized
also: Your next sick leave might be your last.

2. Intense Confidential High-Level Meetings

Of course, increased meetings with upper management could signal a new business venture, an acquisition, your promotion, or some other good news. It could also signal an impending layoff.

All you have to do is call a member of one of your local power bases and ask. Whatever the news, he'll know. If he doesn't, he won't stop until he finds out. Roaming around the personnel or finance departments with benefit or payroll questions can help also. They're usually preoccupied with the information gathering and reporting these calisthenics require. The pensive, worried looks on their faces are a further indication.

Some knowledge of the history of your employer will enable you to make a remarkably accurate prognosis of how he will react to a loss of business. This can be useful in anticipating the signs of a developing crisis. It's like someone who is overweight . . . he crash diets . . . he gorges. Some employers are more susceptible, just like some people.

Fortunately, there is usually considerable time before the axe falls in this situation, because political maneuvering, departmental restructuring, learning duties, evaluating the consequences, and justifying the decisions require time. It's usually a slow, painful committee process.

If you have done your homework by aligning with power brokers, you'll probably avoid being thrown in that pile tragically known as "deadwood."

3. Musical Chairs

Changes in assignments are usually an indication of instability. However, this game of musical chairs is often publicized like a wedding procession. To read the "company press," you would think everyone was being promoted. It's amazing how many employees don't know when a major cutback is in progress! Call it what they will: in musical chairs, someone is always out. Even if you're in the wedding party, there's cause for concern.

If you find the company phone directory is unusually inaccurate or the changes outweigh the original, you should investigate. When you dial a wrong extension, ask what happened to the party you were calling. If the answer doesn't satisfy you, ask the switchboard operator. If you're still not satisfied, tell the personnel department that you need to discuss company business with the former employee. Their failure to give you the phone number may tell you all you need to know. If you receive it, you can call him. Doing your investigating by telephone helps you to remain anonymous. No need to blow your cover.

If you see empty desks or calendars that haven't been turned, casually ask the others who are left. Be suspicious of leaves of absence, extended field assignments, and consulting arrangements with ex-employees. Then you can call the switchboard operator, etc. Wait until you return to your office, though.

This routine vigilance may really help you protect yourself.

4. Changes in Recruiting Efforts

If your employer advertises in the newspaper regularly, and you notice an abrupt shift to smaller or no insertions, a mass hiring freeze may be starting. Layoffs may not be far behind.

When you see a job that looks a lot like yours in a "blind ad" you might ask a friend to respond with a super resume. You shouldn't but you *might*. Your employer shouldn't but he *may have*. This is a perfectly legal and safe way to find out.

Visits from "outplacement consultants" are another clue. Unless the word is out, they can generally be recognized by their sales-type personalities and their unwillingness to discuss their services. Conservative suits on men and women are the standard uniform—dark, like you wear to a funeral. Business cards usually read "Somebody & Associates, Management Consultants."

If you've developed good rapport with a placement service or two, they might be way ahead of you in knowing what's going on. Your counselor can find out fast enough by soliciting a job order for your job. It's amazing how personnel types will open up with recruiters. They just can't resist the temptation to discuss openings or "closings." A few "insider" questions by the recruiter starts the flow of information. Again, a perfectly legal, no-risk maneuver. (Of course, if you *receive* a recruiting call, finding out the source of the referral might also confirm your suspicions. It's a common tactic known as "sell don't tell.")

These techniques can also be used if you see a similar job listed on the bulletin board or elsewhere.

5. Repeated Closed-Door Meetings between your Boss and the Personnel Manager

If business is stable, private sessions between your boss and the personnel manager could be a reading of "The Book"—your personnel folder. How do you know? By the way your boss looks, speaks, and acts.

Watch the eyes. If there's less eye contact, he hasn't been arranging your reserved parking space. The words "we," "our," or "us" may be used in the same sentence with "you." That indicates you're on the outside looking in. The number of inquiries about the progress of your work may also rise or fall sharply, depending upon whether more evidence is being gathered or the decision has already been made.

If you notice that you are sitting across the desk more, instead of at your boss's side, you're losing the game.

Your boss's secretary or assistant will also probably

know. If they haven't been asked their opinion, they may have been told. If your boss tries to hide it, they *definitely* know! When you're reasonably sure the axe is being sharpened, ask them (*not* your boss). Here's a possible way: "Can I ask you something in confidence?" (Listen attentively for an affirmative reply.) "Do you think *(your boss's name)* is happy with my work?"

As my grandmother used to say, "Better a quick pain." Forewarned is forearmed.

6. Requests for Documentation

Interest in status reports and job descriptions always increases when someone is about to be canned. It's a barometer that is remarkably accurate. Bosses and boss's bosses who trust you don't need formal status reports. Ones who can justify what you're doing don't need job descriptions. Furnishing either of these rarely changes their feelings. And you know what a lack of trust and confidence means.

7. A Reduction in the Number and Importance of Duties

Usually fewer duties, but sometimes just less important ones. A drop in the number of "urgent" phone messages, confidential inter-office envelopes and questions in the hall may mean a drop of the axe.

An extension of this is when your boss starts short-circuiting the chain of command and conferring directly with your subordinates. Sometimes you'll just lose your stripes, but usually it's your entire job. Objecting only accelerates the process.

8. Objections to Expense Reimbursement

A fairly accurate measure of your credibility and acceptance is the way your expense reports are handled. If they were approved routinely, and you are now defending the items, beware.

9. Curtailment of Other Reimbursement

As with expense reports, use of company cars, payment of gas allowances, per diem advances, memberships, subscriptions, educational reimbursement, and other benefits requiring prior approval are generally a measure of your value. A change for the worse is usually more personal than just an overall economy measure.

If you are unsure, check with someone in the accounting department about the "guidelines" that are used, just so you know "how to prepare the reports." You'll find out soon enough whether the policy has changed.

10. Avoidance by Co-workers

Like midlife was a communicable disease. "Safety in numbers" is what keeps many co-worker relationships alive. If you find them doing things without asking your opinion, going to lunch without you, ridiculing or insulting you, and acting as though they know something you don't, they might. It's usually not something good. Their stares bring you face-to-face with a fundamental layoff rule:

If you think you have many friends, you might not have any.

Asking the wrong co-worker directly can be a big mistake, since you don't know which side of the axe he may be on if it falls. Pick a reliable source, and say something positive like "I'm really looking forward to working on the *(name of project)* job." If he looks away or changes the subject, he's telling you. He might even confess and offer some suggestions. In any event, if you are careful, you won't be jeopardizing your position.

If you're itching slightly right now, your subconscious has probably already noticed at least one of these symptoms. Think about it. If you recognize more than one . . .

TREATMENT

1. Equal Employment Opportunity Laws

If you believe you can do so with a straight face (apparently smiling didn't work):

a. Look around for something you don't like (a raise that should have been yours, a promotion that passed you over, a derogatory remark that someone in management made, etc.). Easy so far, ay?
b. Connect it with something about yourself that relates to age, medical condition, physical handicap, or sex.

Once you have done so, the trick is to sound like you've consulted with the authorities or an attorney. You'll need some Legalese to sharpshoot and crap shoot with. Its effectiveness is explained by John Striker and Andrew Shapiro in their practical book, *Super Threats:*

> You want to sound detached, calculating and inexorable . . . The beauty of such turgid phrases is their numbing impact; they just hammer away at the senses . . . [of] the typical insecure bureaucrat or the shaky executive that just wants to play it safe.[8]

You probably don't want to do any more than just verbally drop one or two on your boss or some other garden variety power broker. The word will get around—the less you say about your plans, the more management will worry about an investigation, adverse publicity, the cost of defense, an order to pay some astronomical award, a shackle on the door, or jail time. Its attorneys won't be too encouraging either, because they're too busy tailoring the corporate straitjackets that these laws require.

If you *really* want to pursue the matter, you can contact one of the 28 regional Equal Employment Opportunity Commission offices or the designated state agency. But remember: If you go too far, you may just be eased out later for some other well-documented reason, and you'll probably be glad someone finally put you out of your mid-life misery.

All right. Here they are:

Accessibility. The provision for entry and exit of handicapped individuals at the employer's place of business.

Adverse impact. The rate of selection in employment decisions (transfers, promotions, relocations, etc.) that works to the disadvantage of a protected class.

Affirmative action plan or program ("AAP"). A formal, written document enumerating the employer's policy, goals, procedures for monitoring compliance, and delegation of authority to implement equal employment opportunity laws.

Aggregate work force. The entire number of employees that provides the basis for affirmative action requirements.

Back pay. Compensation for past economic loss (reduced wages, denied fringe benefits, etc.) that begins when a discriminatory practice occurs and ends when it is corrected.

Bona fide occupational qualification ("BFOQ"). An official consent from a governmental compliance authority to exclude people in a protected class from performing a particular job. It is difficult to obtain, and must be available for review by the aggrieved employees.

Charge of discrimination ("charge"). The formal claim

filed with the Equal Employment Opportunity Commission that begins the investigative process.

Class action. A civil lawsuit filed by members of a protected class alleging discrimination by the employer. It is extremely difficult to prosecute, but mentioning it tends to shake the ivory tower rafters.

Compliance review. The official investigation that occurs as a result of a claim filed with an authorized governmental agency.

Disparate effect. The result of discrimination against members of a protected class.

Equal Employment Opportunity Commission ("EEOC"). The federal compliance authority for discrimination complaints.

EEO-1 Report. An annual report filed with the Equal Employment Opportunity Commission or state regulatory agency. Separates the aggregate work force into protected classes.

Exemplary damages. An extraordinary amount of money awarded in a civil lawsuit against the employer to set an example, thus discouraging others from perpetuating similar discrimination.

Front pay. Compensation for past economic loss (reduced wages, denied fringe benefits, etc.) that begins when a discriminatory practice occurs and ends when the same level of pay has been reached.

Permanent injunction. An order issued after the trial of a civil lawsuit, requiring cessation of a discriminatory practice indefinitely.

Preliminary injunction. An interim order issued in a civil lawsuit, requiring cessation of a discriminatory practice until the trial.

Protected class (or affected class). Groups designated by age, medical condition, physical handicap, sex, race (color), religion (creed), national origin, ancestry, or arrest information. Discriminatory practices against members by employers is unlawful.

Punitive damages. An extraordinary amount of money awarded in a civil lawsuit against the employer to punish him for past discrimination.

Reasonable accommodation. Anything necessary to alter, adjust, or modify the job, condition of employment, or place of business to overcome any objection he might have to the member of a protected class working, or to make it possible for an employee to do so.

Sexual harassment. Sexual advances or retaliation against a member of either sex for refusing to consent to such advances.

Support data. Statistical analysis and other documentation maintained to justify employment practices.

Systemic discrimination. Continued employment policies or practices that, regardless of their intent, have the effect of perpetuating discrimination.

Temporary restraining order ("TRO"). An immediate order issued in a civil lawsuit that ordinarily "self destructs" in a short period of time, requiring cessation of a discriminatory practice until the hearing on the preliminary injunction.

Underutilization. Employment of members of a protected class at a rate below their availability in the labor market.

Utilization analysis. A statistical procedure designed to identify underutilization.

There you have them. Use them wisely; use them well.

2. Wrongful Termination Laws

Historically, equal employment opportunity laws, collective bargaining contracts, and employment agreements have been the only restrictions on the right of your employer to discharge you whenever he pleased. The law has traditionally been that the formation and continuation of a "contract of employment" is nothing more than an oral agreement, expressed or implied, terminable at will by either party.

However, a few years ago the California Supreme Court reviewed the case of *Tameny v. Atlantic Richfield Company,* 47 Cal. App. 3d 167, 164 Cal. Rptr. 839. Gordon Tameny had been employed by ARCO for 15 years and was allegedly terminated because he refused to participate in an illegal scheme to fix retail gasoline prices. Tameny sued ARCO in Superior Court seeking compensatory and punitive damages for the wrongful discharge. ARCO defended the action, contending it could fire him for any reason it wished. The trial judge agreed, and Tameny appealed the matter to the Supreme Court. In rendering its decision, the court stated:

> The courts have been sensitive to the need to protect the individual employee from discriminatory exclusion from the opportunity of employment whether it be by the all-powerful union or the employer.

Several months later, the Superior Court heard pretrial motions in the matter of *Cleary v. American Airlines, Inc.,* 111 Cal. App. 3d 443, 168 Cal. Rptr. 722. Lawrence Cleary, who had been employed by an airline for 18 years, was discharged for theft and leaving his work area without authorization. The employee denied the "just cause" alleged, arguing that since American had established standard operating procedures for investigating reasons for termination, good faith and fair dealing were required. The District Court of Appeals agreed, stating:

> We have indicated herein the continuing trend for recognition by the courts and the legislature of certain implied contract rights to job security necessary to insure social stability in our society.

The list of companies that have already been burned also includes AT&T, Avco, Firestone, IBM, McGraw-Hill, and NCR—a virtual *Who's Who* of corporate giants.

These and other interpretations of the "terminable at will" concept throughout the United States may result in a "due process" approach to severing the employment relationship never before imposed. Tameny, Cleary and almost every other successful party has been middle-aged. This appears to be a major consideration.

Your best bet is to contact the legal department of your state labor law enforcement agency. Their attorneys are extremely knowledgeable and will undoubtedly know whether any statutes have been enacted, or similar cases have been decided regarding wrongful termination. If so, ask for *specific* case names, since they can be used exactly like Legalese. If you are really ambitious, you can also ask for the citations and visit your local law library. A little help from the reference librarian and a few coins in the photocopy machine will allow you to take the cases home, memorize parts of the decisions, and use them as needed.

You shouldn't need to open the layoff survival kit, and the ingredients are strictly Band-Aids. But if they help, so be it.

CHAPTER 6

Re-entering the Job Supermarket: the Midlife Resume

Resumes of people in our age bracket can usually be readily identified. A typical one contains a sales pitch, states an objective, indicates that children are grown, rambles about job functions, is longer than one page, and is prepared by a resume service. Since forms are not used, as with applications, the determination of qualifications is based almost entirely on subjective criteria (color, type, shape, size, length, and other packaging). It also tends to receive one of two responses from employers: rejection, or even worse, silence. There are rubber stamps available through mail order catalogs that state the feelings of most recipients, but they're rarely used.

Your resume shouldn't look like a letter from Father Time to Father Confessor. If it does, the only door it is likely to open is the one on your mailbox.

The resume is a screening device that enables a busy interviewer to eliminate candidates as quickly and painlessly as possible. In fact, requiring them becomes a matter of survival before long. This means that for most applicants, it is the first mine on the battlefield.

However, a properly drafted midlife resume can be indispensable to *insure* an interview! This is because the depth of general life experience acquired through the years can be reduced to specific items that conform to the job requirements. There may be several resumes required, but once you learn the fail-safe format, this is no problem.

There are many books, magazines, and newspaper articles on how to write a resume. Too many, in fact. While they are well-intentioned, they are only marginally helpful. This is because most authors write about what appeals to *them*. The midlife resume has nothing to do with my personal taste in art. It has been refined over 20 years, and has become increasingly successful in being the most likely to take you from the mailbox to the interviewer's office, where we can perform our midlife magic. If you'll stay close, we'll be finished in about 20 minutes, ready for typing in final form.

The five forms that follow are the blocks to build the resume. Take a separate sheet of blank paper and complete the information for each as we go through it. The comments after each will give you the reasons and additional information. Then, we'll transpose the data on the draft.

IDENTIFICATION

full first name*	middle initial*	last name*

full street address**

city	full name of state	zip code

(_____) _____ - _____ (Message)

* Entire name should be capitalized.
** Apartments or condominiums should be designated "No. _____".
Post office boxes are not recommended.

No abbreviations (except your middle initial) should be used.

Unless you *really* have complete privacy at the office, your residence number (including area code) should be used, designated "(Message)." The only major expense you might have is a telephone-answering device, which I highly recommend. Answering services make it appear that you are a professional jobchanger, and can be unreliable, rude, and expensive. Family members make you look like an amateur, and even if a prospective employer is persistent enough to leave a message, you might not receive it. If *you* answer, "Hello!" means "Unemployed Midlifer" or "Desperate Midlifer," which is hardly the way to present yourself. If there's no answer, the round is probably over. So use the answering device.

The message should be recorded in your own voice, and state pleasantly:

> Hello! This is *(first name, last name)*. I regret that I am unable to answer your call at this time. However, if you leave your name, telephone number, and a brief message after the tone, I will return it as soon as possible.
>
> Thank you for calling!

PERSONAL DATA

Health:	Excellent
Marital Status:	_____
	"Single" or "Married"
Height:	_____' _____"
Weight:	_____ lbs.

This should be self-explanatory.

Do not include references to age, sex, race, religion, place of birth, or citizenship. A photograph should be included only if you are a female or minority *and* you know that the employer is actively engaged in recruiting under an affirmative action plan. While consideration of applicants based upon health, height, weight, and marital status is technically illegal, the absence of any personal data on a resume is a midlife giveaway. Placing it elsewhere on the resume just makes it more obvious.

EDUCATION

_____, _____,
degree (if any)   institution

_____, _____
honors (if any)   last year

_____, _____,
degree (if any)   institution

_____, _____
honors (if any)   last year

_____, _____,
degree (if any)   institution

_____, _____
honors (if any)   last year

_____, _____
certification (if any)   year

Start with the highest credential related to the job you seek, and then continue with those items that are less relevant. Do not include the date any credential was received or dates of attendance. The number of years of attendance is marginally acceptable. Examples are: Licensed Building Contractor; Master of Arts Degree in Journalism, Texas State University; Bachelor of Arts Degree, Chapman College, etc.

Career-related affiliations should be used if possible. However, responsible positions in voluntary organizations demonstrate leadership ability and general competence, so should also be considered. Examples are: Vice President of Detroit Chapter, Association of Data Processing Specialists; Member of National Management Association; Past President of Arlington Lions Club, etc.

AFFILIATION

_____ ,	_____
office or title	organization
_____ ,	_____
office or title	organization
_____ ,	_____
office or title	organization
_____ ,	_____
office or title	organization

EXPERIENCE
Present (or Most Recent) Employer

_____	_____
year	identification
to	(do not name if presently employed)
_____	_____
year or	job title
"Present"	
	_____
	most significant responsibility*
	_____
	_____
	next most significant responsibility*
	_____
	_____
	next most significant responsibility*
	_____
	_____
	next most significant responsibility*
	_____
	_____
	next most significant responsibility*

* Each sentence should begin with a positive, action verb.

This is known as a *chronological* resume. You may be using a *functional* (rhymes with "*flunk*tional") resume that generalizes and combines your duties. A midlife mistake, since people who are hiring are used to application forms that generally follow a reverse chronological format. It is virtually impossible to prepare a functional resume without appearing that you are editorializing and hiding the facts.

Just identify the most recent employer with something like this:

> 1978   Medium-sized Manufacturing Company
>   to   Dallas, Texas
> Present

Then number three or four of your most significant duties, starting each item with a positive, action verb like

Accelerated	Assembled	Compiled
Accepted	Attained	Completed
Achieved	Audited	Composed
Acted	Averted	Computed
Acquired	Bought	Conceived
Adopted	Budgeted	Concentrated
Addressed	Built	Conceptualized
Administered	Calculated	Concluded
Advanced	Centralized	Conducted
Advised	Certified	Conserved
Affected	Chartered	Consolidated
Analyzed	Checked	Constructed
Anticipated	Classified	Consummated
Applied	Coached	Controlled
Appointed	Collaborated	Converted
Arbitrated	Collected	Coordinated
Arranged	Combined	Corrected
Ascertained	Communicated	Counseled

Created
Decentralized
Decided
Decreased
Defined
Delivered
Demonstrated
Designed
Detailed
Detected
Determined
Developed
Devised
Diagnosed
Directed
Discovered
Dispensed
Displayed
Disproved
Distributed
Diverted
Edited
Eliminated
Employed
Enforced
Established
Estimated
Evaluated
Examined
Executed
Explained
Expanded
Expedited
Experimented
Figured
Filed

Followed
Forecasted
Formed
Formulated
Founded
Gathered
Gave
Generated
Guided
Handled
Headed
Helped
Hired
Identified
Illustrated
Implemented
Improved
Improvised
Increased
Influenced
Informed
Initiated
Innovated
Inspected
Installed
Instituted
Instructed
Insured
Integrated
Interceded
Interpreted
Interviewed
Introduced
Invented
Inventoried
Investigated

Judged
Justified
Kept
Launched
Learned
Lectured
Led
Located
Logged
Maintained
Managed
Marketed
Maximized
Measured
Mediated
Met
Minimized
Modernized
Monitored
Motivated
Negotiated
Observed
Obtained
Offered
Operated
Ordered
Organized
Originated
Packaged
Participated
Passed
Perceived
Performed
Persuaded
Pioneered
Planned

Prepared
Prescribed
Presented
Prevented
Processed
Procured
Produced
Programmed
Projected
Promoted
Protected
Provided
Publicized
Published
Purchased
Raised
Read
Realized
Reasoned
Received
Reconciled
Recommended
Recruited
Reduced
Referred
Regulated
Rejected
Related
Rendered
Renegotiated
Reorganized

Repaired
Reported
Represented
Researched
Resolved
Responded
Restored
Retrieved
Reversed
Reviewed
Revised
Revitalized
Saved
Scheduled
Selected
Separated
Served
Set
Settled
Showed
Simplified
Sold
Solved
Sorted
Sought
Specified
Staffed
Standardized
Streamlined
Strengthened
Studied

Summarized
Supervised
Supplied
Supported
Surveyed
Symbolized
Synthesized
Systematized
Tabulated
Taught
Terminated
Tested
Traded
Trained
Translated
Traveled
Treated
Trimmed
Tutored
Undertook
Unified
United
Upgraded
Used
Utilized
Varied
Verified
Weighed
Won
Worked
Wrote

EXPERIENCE (Cont'd.)
Former Employer

_____ year to	_____ name of employer
	_____ job title
_____ year	_____ most significant responsibility*
	_____
	_____ next most significant responsibility*
	_____
	_____ next most significant responsibility*
	_____
	_____ next most significant responsibility*
	_____
	_____ next most significant responsibility*

* Each sentence should begin with a positive, action verb.

The second most recent employer can be disclosed, and then follow the same procedure that you used for the first employer. Combine and omit short-term employment. It's not necessary to list everything you've done, or even every place you've done it. You're not applying for a security clearance, you're just applying for a job!

Undoubtedly, you noticed that the experience worksheet is similar to the job number form we used in Chapter 3. Of course, you can modify your earlier inventory for the resume preparation.

There you have it! No, I didn't forget about a statement

of your abilities, well-adjusted personality, career objective, current salary, salary requirements, or gorgeous children. It's just that they are not found on a fail-safe midlife resume.

Now that you have completed the information, transpose it on one or two sheets of paper in the following form:

_____ ___. _____
_____ _____
_____, _____ _____
(___) ___-_____ (Message)

PERSONAL DATA:
  Health: Excellent   _Height:_ __'__"
  Marital Status: _____   _Weight:_ _____ lbs.

EDUCATION:
  _____, _____;
  _____, _____;
  _____, _____

AFFILIATION:
  _____, _____; _____,
  _____; _____, _____
  _____

EXPERIENCE: _____
  _____   _____
    to   _____
  _____   _____
                   _____
                   _____
                   _____
                   _____
                   _____

  _____   _____
    to   _____

_____   _____
               _____
               _____
               _____
               _____
               _____

REFERENCES: Personal and professional references are
               available. They will be furnished upon
               request, once mutual interest has been
               established.

You will note that a certain statement regarding references is being used. It should be copied exactly at the end
of your draft. References should be cultivated, cherished,
and forewarned. This is a way to make sure that you retain
their important assistance, and coach them properly.

Your draft should now be typed or printed on medium-
to heavy-weight white or ivory paper, with black ink; conservative, medium-sized typeface should be used. My personal preferences are Press Roman type if printed or
Courier if typed with a carbon ribbon. Varying the type-
faces, boldness, and underlining will increase the interest.
Copies should be sharp and clean.

If the five items fill more than one letter-sized page with
a one-inch margin, you simply must reduce "Personal
Data," "Education," or "Affiliation." Statistically, each additional page reduces the chances of a favorable response
by 35 percent. The margin not only looks businesslike, it
conveniently allows a busy interviewer to add his written
comments.

In final form, the resume looks like this:

DAVID L. BAKER
35 Ridgeway Street
Hartford, Connecticut 37321
(203) 839-2601 (Message)

PERSONAL DATA:
Health:	Excellent	*Height:* 5'10"
Marital Status:	Single	*Weight:* 160 lbs.

EDUCATION:
Registered Professional Engineer; Master of Science Degree in Business Administration, Pennsylvania State University; Bachelor of Arts Degree, University of California at Los Angeles

AFFILIATION:
Vice President of Connecticut Chapter, Engineering Management Society; Member of American Association of Business Executives; Past President of Bridgeport Neighborhood Watch Program

EXPERIENCE:

1978
to
Present

Medium-sized Manufacturing
Company
Hartford, Connecticut
Manager of Operations
1. Supervised approximately 50 employees, directing overall company administration and operations.
2. Prepared a comprehensive customer service manual that reduced troubleshooting time by over 50%.
3. Surveyed data-processing equipment and negotiated the contract for its purchase.
4. Improved the clerical work flow significantly, receiving the annual Most Valuable Employee Award.

1974
to
1978

Allied Machine Parts, Inc.
Hidden Valley, New York
Senior Engineer
1. Developed the prototype for a valve that became a major product manufactured by the company.

2. Monitored the status of the parts inventory, coordinating with the purchasing, operations, and manufacturing departments to maintain adequate supplies.
3. Supervised the technical support personnel in the absence of the chief engineer.

REFERENCES: Personal and professional references are available. They will be furnished upon request, once mutual interest has been established.

or this:

SUSAN R. SHAW
206 Butler Avenue
Phoenix, Arizona 40161
(612) 587-0934 (Message)

PERSONAL DATA:
Health: Excellent   *Height:* 5′6″
Marital Status: Married   *Weight:* 125 lbs.

EDUCATION:
Certificate of Completion, Career Business College; High School Diploma, Devon High School

AFFILIATION:
Vice President, Executive Secretaries Association; Member, National Office Administrators League; Past President, Devon Community Service Program

EXPERIENCE:
1976   Major Electronics Manufacturing
to   Company
Present   Phoenix, Arizona
Office Administrator
1. Supervised the clerical staff, including participation in employee performance reviews.

2. Assisted with the compilation of a detailed office procedures manual.
3. Expedited distribution of product brochures, press releases and interdivision bulletins.

1973
to
1976

Roberts Development, Inc.
Tucson, Arizona
Senior Secretary

1. Prepared field reports from sales representatives.
2. Coordinated the purchase of office supplies, ordering from vendors when necessary.
3. Arranged travel for corporate officers, including scheduling meetings, transportation and lodging.
4. Trained clerical employees in use of office machines.

REFERENCES:

Personal and professional references are available. They will be furnished upon request, once mutual interest has been established.

or, for a soon-to-be-pleasantly-surprised midlife woman with four children, recently divorced, lacking any paid work experience, but active in the Girl Scouts, like this:

ELAINE B. OLSON
3 Amherst Circle, No. 704
Santa Monica, California 96572
(213) 386-5421 (Message)

PERSONAL DATA:

Health: Excellent   *Height:* 5'3"
Marital Status: Single   *Weight:* 120 lbs.

EDUCATION:

Business Courses, Santa Monica College; Word Processor Training, Western Data Processing Institute; High School Diploma, Los Angeles High School

AFFILIATION:
Parent-Teacher Coordinating Council; Recreation and
Parks Program; Community Development Organization;
Civic Activities

EXPERIENCE:

1980 to Present	National Youth Assistance Organization Los Angeles, California Director

1. Implemented a complete system of
   reporting between chapters, to improve communication and maximize use of equipment.
2. Supervised a field staff responsible
   for conducting local and regional
   projects.
3. Led a successful drive to re-estab-
   lish necessary dialogue with civic
   and business leaders.
4. Motivated the directors of other
   chapters to devise new ways to obtain contributions from sponsors.

1976 to 1980	Community Improvement Program Santa Monica, California Administrator

1. Initiated the preparation of an operations manual for use by inspec-
   tors.
2. Strengthened the existing public relations activities, including interface
   with media buying service.
3. Prepared reports for city and state
   agencies to ensure their continued
   support.
4. Streamlined internal paper flow so
   that the efforts of staff workers
   would be maximized.

REFERENCES:	Personal and professional references are available. They will be furnished upon request, once mutual interest has been established.

You'll notice that all of these resumes are simple and straightforward. They are designed to convey information; it is a mistake to think that they should be unusual or to attempt to overwhelm the reader. If you want to do more, a cover letter can be an excellent marketing device to personalize your communication. It should be used instead of a statement of career objectives on the resume and can set you apart favorably from other midlife applicants. It can also be used to identify the name of your referral.

Your homework should include a phone call to the company to find out the correct spelling of the interviewer's name and title, full company name and address, and other details. This really makes a difference in your presentation.

High quality white or ivory paper should be used, and should match the resume as closely as possible. The letter should be typed with a conservative, medium-sized face, using a black carbon ribbon.

1. ADDRESS LINE
   The full company name and address (no abbreviations), full name of the interviewer, and full title should be used. These make you look thorough and professional.
2. SUBJECT LINE
   "Re: Interview for the Position of *(title)*." This zeros in on the contents and dresses up the letter.
3. GREETING
   "Dear Mr./Ms. *(last name)*." "Miss" or "Mrs." should not be used unless you know the interviewer does so. First

names are out of the question, even if they were used during an earlier conversation.

4. OPENING

    a. "I am responding to your advertisement that appeared in *(name of newspaper)* on *(date)* for the position of *(title)*."

    b. "It was a pleasure speaking with you today to discuss the position of *(title)* with *(name of company)*. As we discussed, I have enclosed a copy of my resume."

    c. "In a recent conversation with *(first and last name of referral)*, it was suggested that I forward a copy of my resume to you."

It is important to refer immediately to either the position or the referral. This will make it easier for the interviewer to identify you. There's that first impression again!

Now, you can be less formal and discuss your common goal. Sales trainers call this "sizzle." But if it exceeds two short paragraphs, you'll call it "fizzle."

5. BODY

    a. "My qualifications appear to match the requirements for the position. In particular, _____ _____ _____. Therefore, it sounds like an excellent opportunity."

    b. "From our discussion, and the fine reputation of your organization, it appears that the *(title)* position would enable me to fully utilize my background in _____ _____."

    c. "From my discussion with *(first name of referral)* and other information I have obtained, *(name of company)* seems to have the kind of environment I have been seeking. Therefore, I would undoubtedly be able to contribute significantly to its goals, through _____ _____ _____."

6. CLOSING
   a. "While I have been considering other situations, I have deferred a decision until we can meet personally. Therefore, your prompt reply would be greatly appreciated."
   b. "It appears to be an exciting opportunity, and I look forward to hearing from you regarding an appointment for a personal interview."
   c. "The *(title)* position and *(name of company)* are exactly what I have been seeking, and I hope to hear from you within the next week."
7. SALUTATION
   a. "Sincerely,"
   b. "Very truly yours,"
   c. "Best regards,"

Here is an example of how a completed letter should look, accompanying the first resume:

DAVID L. BAKER
35 Ridgeway Street
Hartford, Connecticut 37321
(203) 839-2601

January 10, 1985

Standard Information Systems, Inc.
15779 Industrial Parkway
Wheaton, Connecticut 37325

Attn: Richard M. Carlton, Executive Vice President

Re: Interview for the Position of Operations Manager

Dear Mr. Carlton:

It was a pleasure speaking with you today to discuss the position of Operations Manager with Standard Information Systems, Inc. As we discussed, I have enclosed a copy of my resume.

From our discussion, and the fine reputation of your organization, it appears that the Operations Manager position would enable me to utilize my background in implementing an effective cost control system. In addition, my experience in purchasing data-processing equipment at Telecommunications International last year would assist you in making the transition at Standard. As a result of implementing my suggestions, the company was able to reduce clerical overhead by 40 percent.

While I have been considering other situations, I have deferred a decision until we can meet personally. Therefore, your prompt reply would be greatly appreciated.

Very truly yours,

DAVID L. BAKER

DLB:ebs
Enclosure

When Justice Frank Richardson retired from the California Supreme Court recently, he was asked about the most common mistake made by lawyers. His reply was:

Scattering their fire. To the extent the lawyer can, he or she should go for the jugular . . . It is useful for the lawyer to learn what particular areas will interest the court. Otherwise the judge is going to hear things that he's already decided one way or the other or that he deems inconsequential. If the lawyer can, he should try to divine where the target issues are and focus on that. A rifle rather than a shotgun is more effective.[9]

I rest my case.

CHAPTER 7

Re-entering the Job Supermarket: the Consultant Phone Call

The "Consultant Phone Call" is the midlifer's key to obtaining as many interviews as possible. Only then can the interviews be converted into offers.

About a third of the people our age who have problems re-entering the world of work or changing jobs don't know how to arrange an interview. The comments, "I've never looked for a job before," "I never thought I'd have to work again," or "Employers have always called me" head the list of reasons.

There are more applicants in traditional fields now than jobs available. If you have been displaced by technology, you need no further convincing that "structural unemployment" is also occurring. Passive jobseeking has become a contradiction in terms.

Another third of the midlifers looking for a job did so when employers were satisfied with anyone possessing a discernible pulse. My office was known as the "body shop." I would pick up the phone, and some supervisor would bellow, "Hello! Body shop? Send me four bodies." They thought we *manufactured* applicants! Now the problem has become how to screen them out gracefully and legally.

The final third are those who are frightened of interviewing because of their midlife status. Whether these folks avoided it because they were too young ("inexperienced") or for some other reason will never be known. The symptoms range from simple discomfort to advanced apoplexy. If you are in this category, simply visualize successful interviews (real or imagined) while in a relaxed state. This works wonders when you are in the process of scheduling them.

The key to obtaining interviews is to view the *appointment* as an end in itself, not just a means to an end. If you do, you will be overcoming the self-imposed obstacles in your way while you're getting to the bridge. Crossing it is covered in the next chapter.

Personal contacts (business associates, former supervisors and co-workers, and friends) are the primary networking source to obtain interviews, as we'll see in Chapter 9. Although the number of contacts would seem to increase with age, this is not the case for the two largest segments of the middle-age jobseeking population: Those who haven't changed jobs recently and those who are re-entering the job market after an extended absence. If you're one of them, your easiest entry to a job interview—and especially to the unadvertised jobs—is to market yourself as a "consultant."

Before you can join the "advice squad," however, bear in mind those factors that are the hallmark of the consultant image:

- An age of 40 to 70.
- A judicious look on your face (when you're not smiling, of course).
- An ultra-conservative dress or suit.
- An ability to pronounce at least 20 of the latest "buzz words" in your field (trade publications are the best place to learn them).

- A brochure about your expertise and services (in addition to a fail-safe resume).
- A business card.
- A local business license (if required).

The reason consulting is so easy to discuss is that there is almost no expense or risk to the "client." According to the United States Chamber of Commerce, up to 36 percent of a typical business payroll is spent on administration alone. This is not surprising when you consider the recordkeeping, bookkeeping, cash flow management, payroll taxes, paid holidays, paid vacations, paid sick leave, paid insurance, and paid everything else.

As an "independent contractor" rather than employee, there's no concern about you running to the EEOC or state agency with an age, medical condition, physical handicap, or sex discrimination complaint. No concern with group medical, workers' compensation, or disability claims either. You are issued a "1099" (an Internal Revenue Service form) at the end of the year and pay your own taxes.

This arrangement is not available for hourly ("non-exempt") jobs, unless you are engaged in the activity on a free-lance basis, and various restrictions exist. A call to your state labor department will be all you'll need to find out whether you are eligible.

Telephone solicitation is the best way to obtain an appointment. Simply look in the Yellow Pages in any field you like with an appointment calendar open, and start in the "A" 's. The beauty of the "consultant" routine is that it postures you immediately to talk to the hiring authority without alienating the personnel type. It is an accepted practice for consultants to discuss "projects" directly with those responsible for them. Even the personnel field has its cadre of management development, training, human factors, wage and salary, recruiting, outplacement, insurance, pension, employee benefits, safety, communications, labor relations, and other consultants. Would they speak with a young employment interviewer? Not if they have a business card!

The usual telephobia will subside after a few calls. It's easy to sound knowledgeable when you don't understand the situation. Then, as a consultant and senior member of the human race, you will have a tendency to be overbearing. Possibly your victim hasn't learned those 20 buzz words, so be careful not to oversell.

A competent advisor listens well, probes, asks questions, uses the same vocabulary as the client, and avoids "shooting from the lip." The appointment is an *end in itself*. The call is the means. It's usually about five minutes in length. Any longer will reduce the chances of a personal meeting. You're interviewing, not arranging, if the conversation lingers. More investigation is needed for an interview. This is how the voice of experience sounds:

Receptionist:	Good morning, Company X.
You:	Hi. What's the name of your Director of Finance?
Receptionist:	We don't have a Director of Finance. Would you like to speak to our Chief Accountant?
You:	Yes, please. Who is it?
Receptionist:	Gail Davis is her name.
You:	Thank you.
Receptionist:	One moment, please. I'll ring . . .
Secretary:	Accounting. May I help you?
You:	Hi. Ms. Davis, please.
Secretary:	May I tell her who's calling?
You:	*(first name) (last name).*
Secretary:	May I tell her what it's regarding?
You:	Sure. I wanted to speak to her about your cost control system.

Secretary:	Is there something I can help you with?
You:	No, I'm sorry. I really must speak with Gail.
Secretary:	Just a moment . . . I'll see if she's available.
Supervisor:	Gail Davis.
You:	Hi, Gail. My name is *(first name) (last name)*. I'm a consultant in the finance area, and would like to discuss how I might assist with improving your cost control system.
Supervisor:	Our system works fine. Well . . . there are a few things that could use improvement.
You:	I'm really familiar with this, and have been very successful in reducing costs with clients. What areas do you see as needing improvement?
Supervisor:	Inventory control has really become a problem. We're just unable to keep track of our costs!
You:	Your costs? Why?
Supervisor:	Well, our production control group has not been following up on status reports.
You:	An objective appraisal can often help to straighten this problem out.
Supervisor:	Really? I never thought of that.
You:	I'll be in your area on a consulting assignment later this week. Why don't I stop by to see you at nine on Thursday morning?
Supervisor:	I'm on a very limited budget. What do you charge?
You:	Why don't we see whether I can be of assistance first. There won't be any charge at all. If I can do you some good, we can discuss it further. However, it appears we'll be able to reduce the costs substantially at Company X without a major change.

Supervisor:	OK, you're on.
You:	Thanks. I estimate we'll be about an hour.
Supervisor:	Fine.
You:	I'm looking forward to meeting you! See you then.
Supervisor:	Sounds good. Bye.
You:	Goodbye.

While the call can start differently and take an infinite number of turns, you are controlling the dialogue. It should *be* a dialogue, *not* two monologues. Listen actively, but don't give away your valuable advice when clients are willing to pay for it. How much is "too much"? Anything beyond "just enough." You're giving away the sample, not selling the product.

Abraham Lincoln said it, and every lawyer knows it:

Your time and advice are your stock in trade.

Fee or free—which will it be?

You may have to leave a few messages before you swing into action. If the supervisor calls back, *always* be courteous but too busy to talk. Ask if you can return the call in a "few minutes." This makes you appear in demand. It then enables you to organize your thoughts, review your notes, drink a cup of coffee (please), and relax. Then by initiating the call, your control position is increased.

In studying the Consultant Phone Call, you'll note that the emphasis is on helping someone else. We are utilizing one of the most basic success principles ever discovered:

You will get what you want, if you give others what they want.

The call also considers the natural insecurity of anyone who depends upon another for emotional and financial support. It is a success principle etched in bronze on a plaque in our office:

There's a big difference between advising and assisting.

The call utilizes another success principle that makes it so dramatically effective:

Don't mention you are looking for a job.

The last thing you want to say to a supervisor who is in trouble, whether real or imagined, is that you intend to replace her. In fact, you want to make her feel that you will be like George Burns in *Oh, God!* An invisible miracle worker. The fact is, you probably *will* be!

You can vary the call if you want to start by looking for a job. If you do, be careful *not* to mention your midlife stature to an interviewer or hiring authority. Invariably, this is interpreted as "You wouldn't want to hire me anyway!" It's irrelevant, and if considered as a factor, illegal. You might be given the appointment just so the employer can protect itself and drop the standard "equal employment" age rejection letter on you: "We're sorry, you're overqualified." Ask for an application to be mailed to your home, so you can type it neatly in advance.

As you go down the alphabet, making notes on the Yellow Pages and calendar, you will notice that you become more adept at finessing around the front-liners. You want to be completely honest, not only for moral reasons. Misrepresenting destroys your self-respect. This is conveyed in your delivery. Midlife isn't endlife . . . many know it's often "beginlife." Start out believing in yourself, forgetting about your age, the time of day, the day of the week, the area code, the last call, an errand to run, or any other excuse to procrastinate. The world awaits the voice of experience.

For a few dollars, you can buy a suction-cup telephone pickup from any electronics store to plug into any tape recorder. This invaluable device is used by many placement counselors to perfect their presentation, and check the accuracy of their notes. When used for training, the feedback of this technique under actual conditions is unequaled by any other training method. As long as the tape is used solely by you, it is within the limits of the law. You'll be proud of your performance within a few days, but resist the temptation to blast the conversation in the employer's lobby when you arrive. You've already got the supervisor's attention.

An appointment around one hour after the start of business is best for this caper. Unlike standard employment interviews with personnel types, a second appointment after lunch is a mistake. Supervisors who are overworked are often behind schedule and already irritable by noon. And it's worse after lunch—even energetic midlifers tend to run down at sundown. This will inhibit your ability to leave with a job (oops! "consulting assignment"). Let those supercharged morning hours work their magic. Schedule a meeting an hour after business starts, since it gives the supervisor time to settle down to business and, most important, it gives you time to arrive and "scope out" the situation in advance.

I hope you're beginning to see that the "hidden job market" isn't hidden at all. It's the *applicants* who are hiding! It should be called the "obvious job market." How much more obvious could it be than inside every telephone?

You can prove the fallacy of chasing help-wanted advertisements for yourself. By the time an employer is *paying* for responses in a help-wanted ad, you're just part of an amorphous mass at the wide end of a funnel. That's the phenomenon you see on the news every so often—500 workers outside some assembly plant applying for one job.

It makes interesting news, but that's not how the game is played.

Placement services wouldn't stay in business if they just canvassed help-wanted ads or waited for employers to call them. They know the secret, and now you do also. Penetrate *before* the job is officially available. That's relying on human nature. A very reliable thing.

"HELP AVAILABLE" ADVERTISING

The Consultant Phone Call is a proven technique, but before we leave the subject of interview scheduling, one other deserves honorable mention. It is the advertising campaign to augment your telephone solicitation campaign. A "help-available" classified advertisement in a metropolitan newspaper is the reciprocal of a "help-wanted" ad, and might read like this:

ENGINEERING EXECUTIVE

Proven ability. Presently vice president of diversified manufacturing company. Seeking executive position in:
* Economic Feasibility
* Planning, Mergers, Acquisitions
* Patent Review, Licensing
* Top Corporate Management
Box 3780, *Daily Sun*

or this:

DIRECTOR OF MARKETING

Currently employed, seeking position in hi-tech electronics field. Experienced in component selling, merchandising, distributing, planning and advertising. Participated in corporate acquisitions and mergers. Phone (212) 732-0061 or Box 8773, *The Register*.

or even this:

BUYING PROBLEMS?

Experienced purchasing agent looking to assist growing
manufacturing company. Highly qualified in cost reduction
and vendor selection procedures. Immediately available
and willing to relocate for right opportunity. Please reply
to:

P. O. Box 2306
Denver, CO 88521

Since your identity isn't disclosed, it makes no difference whether you are currently employed. If you're looking for consulting assignments, display ads are also a
possibility. They are more expensive but enable you to be
more creative and perhaps elicit more responses.

As you read the help-wanted ads in your field, you will
begin to see a pattern in the requirements and layout.
There are just not that many ways to advertise a certain
type of job! This should be useful in giving you a format
to use. Other help-available ads will also be a valuable
source. If you want to enter a new field, try to pick something in your background that is related. Advertising your
qualifications to become the first midlife astronaut on the
moon will probably get responses only from local space
cadets.

The classified ads are required weekend reading for
employment professionals, even if they are not hiring.
Placement counselors, executive recruiters, and others in
the hiring process will also be in the audience. You may be
surprised how well and how inexpensively your background can be marketed either as a prospective employee
or consultant. Of course, you can experiment with different kinds of jobs. Be ready with a fail-safe resume for each
and a well-drafted cover letter.

Trade journals, newsletters, and related periodicals are

also possibilities, but check lead times. They are usually too long, and therefore these should be considered a secondary source only.

Use of print media advertising is a painless way to let prospective employers know about your capabilities. You may feel slightly commercial doing so, but the United States Supreme Court says it's even acceptable for lawyers. Who are we to argue with the United States Supreme Court? Apply now. No experience required.

Don't take it personally if you are not satisfied with the responses. How could *anyone* take an anonymous mail box personally?

It's safe to assume your appointment is scheduled. Here's how to set up the "Nose-to-Nose Close."

CHAPTER 8

Re-entering the Job Supermarket: the Nose-to-Nose Close

THE PREPARATION

The most important mission has already been accomplished: You have arranged a personal meeting with a potential employer. You should wait for a few hours, and then *anonymously* call another department to gather intelligence about it. Sales, marketing, customer service, public relations, and personnel departments are a natural. These are staff functions and telephone communication is a large part of the job. Even a receptionist or switchboard operator can be extremely helpful if they're not too busy, since their jobs are often the nerve center through which information flows. Since they constantly deal with the general public, they are used to fielding questions. And if they don't know the answers, they can route you to somebody who does. You are asking anonymously, so this is an exception to the rule about not asking the question unless you know the answer mentioned in Chapter 4. It is better to seem ignorant now by asking them than to make foolish mistakes later. Typical questions you should ask are:

1. Where is the business headquartered?
2. Who owns the business?
3. How many facilities does the business have?
4. What divisions does the business have?
5. How many employees does the business have?
6. What are the main products or services of the business?
7. What markets does the business serve?
8. What are the new products or services of the business?
9. What are the annual sales of the business?
10. How long has the business been in operation?

If you like, you can prepare a worksheet with the questions and photocopy it as a guide in sleuthing. Your seasoned sense and sensitivity will crack any employer within a matter of minutes. You can even call several people anonymously, until you're satisfied. This reduces a lot of the fear of the unknown that terrorizes so many midlifers in the interviewing process. Be sure to obtain exact directions to the place where the interview will be held.

If it looks as if you might be cultivating an internal referral, disclose who you are and why you are calling. Comment that you would like to stop by and say "Hello!" when you're there. Keep it low-key because anything beyond that might seem overbearing and jeopardize the chance for a precious third-party testimonial. This can be the most potent kind of entry into any job.

Don't lean on the referral, as midlifers have a tendency to do. The worst that can happen if no "end-run" is made is that you'll mention that you know a co-worker to the supervisor. After the interview, you can call back the referral and listen for a while. *Then* you can lean, if the person seems receptive, by asking him to "put in a good word" for you or otherwise assist. People like to do this; for some, it reflects their desire to help; for others, it reinforces their sense of power; for both, it increases their self-worth.

Most midlifers are surprised at how much can be learned by listening. That's because we don't do it enough. Ironically, when we do, others listen more to us as well, since it's easier to separate the matter from the chatter.

BACK-UP RESEARCH

There is another way to find out about employers, of course, and you can do it by visiting the reference section of your local public library. The shelves and microfilm machines are filled with information on many publicly held and even privately held companies. The most available sources are:

Annual Reports
Business Periodicals Index (H. W. Wilson Company)
Dun and Bradstreet's Million Dollar Directory
Moody's News Reports
Moody's Manuals
Standard and Poor's Register of Corporations Directors, and Executives
Standard and Poor's Corporation Records
Thomas Register of American Manufacturers
MacRae's Blue Book
Value Line Investment Surveys

The trouble with these references is that they are of greater use to a financial investor, and you often have to read between the lines. It's a laborious process, and it lacks the flexibility and opportunity of a line of incisive questioning.

I don't recommend the library procedure, though. Midlife is too short, especially when Ma Bell is so ready, willing, and able to help.

The "Nose-to-Nose Close" depends on what shows. So here goes: Most people agree that first impressions really count. However, they are unaware of how much *more* important they are in midlife jobseeking. This is because those who are hiring are extremely busy and see so many applicants. The *personnel policy* says they're not supposed to discriminate; the *law* says they're not supposed to discriminate; they usually *don't want* to discriminate; and they may *try not* to discriminate. But they discriminate like crazy! In fact, that's what they're paid to do. Stereotyping is the order of the day.

My first job as an interviewer was working for the director of industrial relations of a large company. We outgrew the main building and were relocated to a converted house nearby. His office was in one of the rooms in front, and had a window where he could see the applicants as they walked in. Mine was in the back, since I worked for him. We didn't need resumes, applications, or references to decide who to hire. He would buzz me on the intercom and say, "That one looks good." More often than not, he'd have his way and the person would be hired. It was about as scientific then as it is now.

Therefore, it should come as no surprise that, for many jobs, first impressions mean the difference between success and failure.

Let's look at your looks, nose to toes, and in between.

You should have at least two changes for your interviewing "uniform," and a number of other items should be correct.

MEN

According to almost every image consultant, there is only one way for a midlife man to dress to be offered almost any job.

1. Clothes

a. *Navy blue three-piece suit.*   Wool and wool blends look better and last longer. Solid colors or subdued stripes are preferred. Gray may be worn, but Brooks Brothers has never been able to manufacture natural-shoulder navy blue suits fast enough to meet the demand. Shiny fabrics should be avoided, and no religious, fraternal, or service pins should be worn.

b. *White long-sleeved dress shirt.*   Laundered and starched commercially! Your interviewer won't wear a monogram, and therefore you shouldn't. Collar style should be current, and if French cuffs are worn, cuff links should not reflect any religious, fraternal, or service affiliation. They should also be the same color as your watch, and neither should be larger than necessary.

c. *Dark blue striped tie.*   A contrasting color is acceptable, but the predominant color should be the same as your suit. Silk or other thin fabrics are recommended.

d. *Black over-the-calf hosiery.*   Hairy legs are definitely not elegant. Support hose are terrific when you're an active midlifer, and look identical to the regular kind.

e. *Black dress shoes.*   Almost any style is acceptable as long as they can be polished well and are.

These five items comprise the all-American look in the fashion industry, and it is interesting that its positive effect has been unanimously acclaimed by the specialists.

Beware of fad clothes; more often than not, they'll ruin your chances for the job, and you'll need a new wardrobe when they become obsolete a season later. And beware of frayed or outdated clothes, scuffed shoes, worn jewelry or glasses, and other midlife memorabilia—give them to the

Salvation Army. Look at it this way: They need the job, and you won't get one unless you do.

If you haven't discovered the clothing values at discount, wholesale, and factory-direct outlets, you're in for a pleasant surprise. A revolution in the apparel industry has rendered paying retail prices unnecessary. Almost every major city has a garment district filled with outlets open to the public. The direct-selling, competitive, swap-meet atmosphere makes the buys and selection unbeatable. Cash only is accepted in some cases, so be prepared. Tailors are everywhere, and often charge less than half the usual rates. Wear comfortable shoes, because you will do a lot of walking. If you plan to have tailoring done, wear a shirt and shoes that can provide accurate measurements. The labels might be different or not be there at all, but you won't be wearing your clothes inside-out anyway!

If you require extensive alterations on ready-to-wear clothes, you might check out custom tailors. They are in abundance in garment districts, and the prices are often only slightly higher. The difference in your looks may be well worth it.

2. Hair

Your hair frames your face—and you know what a difference a good picture frame can make to your family portrait! In spite of all the advertising for hair preparations, very few people in midlife condition and style their hair properly. We just do it the same old way, while the styles have changed and the products have improved.

As a daily routine:

a. Shampoo your hair with a natural, pH-balanced formula for your type of hair, containing conditioner. (Natural dandruff-remover shampoos are also available.)

b. Use a separate conditioner compatible with the shampoo.
c. Use a brush and hair dryer simultaneously.
d. Use unscented hair spray instead of creams or oils.

Find a professional stylist. Convenience and friendship are no reasons to choose any professional. Let barbers "barber" someone else. Ask around, find yourself a stylist who can work some magic for you, and let him do so on a regular basis. Your hair should be no longer than the bottom of your neck, and neatly trimmed. A perm is fine.

At midlife it is perfectly natural to have thinning hair or even to be bald. But if you are in an occupation where youthful looks matter, or just want to feel younger, take the lead of over half the middle-age actors (and actresses) and invest in a hairpiece.

It would take an encyclopedia to review the hundreds of variations, and a thesaurus to list the different names for the same things, but all you really need to do is find a specialist who manufactures on the premises, check his references, and be certain that only natural hair is used. You can be grossly overcharged, but if you pay less than $1,000, you're probably better off using a household mop. Stay away from anything that even sounds surgical, or you might end up looking like a midlife Mohawk.

Hairpieces are virtually undetectable if manufactured, maintained, and styled properly.

3. Face

You can have a moustache or beard if it is neatly trimmed, but in most businesses it is not considered an asset.

Your eyeglasses should be a conservative, current style.

4. Hands

A professional manicure is not necessary, but keep your nails trim and clean. A buffer is a good investment, or use clear nail polish. A ring should be simple in design and expensive in looks. A wrist watch doesn't matter as much, since it's out of sight. (Successful midlifers tend to wear gold and eat with silver.)

5. Fragrance

If you use after-shave lotion or cologne, carefully choose one for interviewing. The sense of smell is the most basic of the five senses—a thousand times stronger than the sense of taste. The receptors in the nostrils of your interviewer are directly connected to the part of his brain that is involved with his deepest emotions. You can help or hinder yourself substantially, so it's best to use fragrance sparingly.

WOMEN

1. Clothes

The image consultants don't agree on an interviewing uniform for midlife women. But they do agree that conservatism is essential, and that suits or dresses in basic colors are appropriate.

a. *Avoid:*
   V-necks
   High hemlines
   Jewelry reflecting any religious or organizational affiliation
   Gaudy fashion jewelry
   Oversized handbags

b. *Natural shade full-length stockings.* A variety of sheer support stockings are now available. I understand they are as effective as men's support hosiery.

c. *Leather dress shoes.*   All heel lengths are available, so you should choose one that enables you to approach average height (around 5′5″), but don't use more than a 1½″ heel. This is best for jobseeking and jobkeeping.

Since women's fashions change faster than men's, you will find discount, wholesale and, factory-direct outlets a virtual bonanza of style, selection, and value. The garment district also has many sources for handbags, shoes, and jewelry. Most of the places are even open Saturdays! Bring cash and don't forget to wear comfortable shoes.

2. Hair

As with men, your hair is the frame that adorns your face. Generally, shorter, naturally colored hair is preferred. Longer hairstyles may make daily shampooing impractical, but otherwise the same routine should be used.

Your choice of a hairdresser should be based upon strictly business reasons—the best you can look at the best price. Fortunately, you have many to choose from.

If you want to practice your assertiveness in a very constructive way, visit a local wig salon with an instant camera and a friend. Experiment to your heart's content. Even if your friend doesn't take a picture of you to show your hairdresser, you will be able to explain the best style to him. People in wig salons are used to "lookie-loos," and you might pick up some valuable advice on improving your image. The large department store salons are a great place to visit, since the "consultants" are not paid on a commission basis. In fact, they *love* having someone to talk to.

3. Face

Today's midlife woman wears minimal, understated makeup that looks natural. Since the varieties of makeup and the faces that they cover are so great, I can't give you a list of accurate guidelines. However, makeup or beauty consultants are everywhere—direct sales, home parties, beauty salons, beauty supply stores, cosmetic stores, health food stores, drug stores, department stores, and almost everywhere else you turn.

My suggestion is that you frequent the department stores at slow times (preferably weekdays or evenings) when the hourly paid consultants are looking for "consultees." Tell the person that you are *not* going to buy, only to experiment. Their practical experience with so many items and the information they receive from manufacturers' representatives, customers, and even formal training are invaluable. The makeup areas generally have comfortable chairs and optimum lighting.

The more expensive department stores will not only offer better quality and selection, but the staff will be more knowledgeable and service-oriented. Since the markup in makeup is way up, you should compare prices before you buy.

This project takes a while, and you should allow yourself several sessions at a few stores. Therefore, plan to go alone. You might also buy one of the many self-help beauty books available in almost any bookstore and follow their career-oriented advice.

If you wear earrings, they should match your other jewelry, and be no larger than the size of your earlobe.

There is a wide variety of eyeglasses you can wear, but avoid outdated, oversized, or ostentatious frames.

4. Hands

Your hairdresser may be affiliated with a manicurist. However, there is no reason why you can't buy yourself one of the many manicure kits available. Nails should extend no more than a quarter of an inch past the fingers and be polished in traditional shades, unless something else is customary for the job.

Your watch, bracelet, and ring should match; gold is preferred to silver. Whatever you use should not be gaudy.

5. Fragrance

Cologne or perfume is recommended for women. The selection should be carefully made and changed only rarely, since the subliminal "power of a woman" is being wielded and maintained. As with makeup and dress, *moderation* is the key, but it's not a physical handicap to be attractive and feminine.

For both men and women, regardless of the position, an attaché case is an excellent accessory. It looks businesslike, and identifies you with the interviewer. Dark brown is more popular, but I prefer black for men, since it matches the shoes.

The case should be wide enough to store a small container of instant coffee (or a few regular tea bags), breath spray, deodorant, cologne, nonsmoking tablets (if necessary), a comb or brush, a gold pen with black ink, a legal pad (the kind lawyers use to intimidate), notes on the employer, six extra copies of your resume, a typed application form, and other job-related documents.

Exceptions that prove the rule of conservative dress are few and far between: Highly creative art and entertainment jobs are where they are found. However, looking the part of the job you hope to find is far less powerful than looking the part of the person who will hire you for it. Yes, you can dress differently—if you know what a supervisor in a creative department will be wearing.

Even in fad and fashion industries, personnel professionals tend to be conservative. Their decisions are often made in groups, and to the extent that you vary from middle-age, middle-class, and middle-management values, success in the interview will vary. You can always dress down a little when you arrive. You can't dress up.

Ask any actor:

Look the part, and the part plays itself.

THE CLOSE

All right. You've arrived at the employer's office about an hour early, but don't go in. Remember what I said in the last chapter about allowing time to scope out the situation when the appointment was arranged.

THE FIRST HALF-HOUR

The first half-hour is strictly for an unguided sightseeing tour around the area and acclimating yourself to the surroundings.

If it is merely a suite in an ordinary office building, just casually walk or drive around the area, staying as relaxed and as comfortable as you can. Get a feel for the area, take time for a cup of coffee, and be friendly to the people you meet, but stay away from anything or anyone that will distract you for more than a minute or so.

If it is a building entirely occupied by the business, BINGO! Go right in and scope away. Look at bulletin boards and office directories. Observe the people. Strike up a short conversation with the security guard (another highly credible source for everything from directions to work habits of the inmates). If you can be inconspicuous, let yourself eavesdrop on conversations about the employer in the halls.

Incidentally, I have recommended coffee at this time

because you will naturally reach a psychomotor peak as the time arrives to greet the interviewer. With midlifers, this tends to drop like a depth charge after about 20 minutes. Adrenaline does this.

After age 40, our basal metabolism lowers by about two percent per decade. That's why you may not feel as chipper as when you were younger. It's only a slight difference, but *this* is the competitive edge you can lose if you're not careful. If you don't want to start mumbling and shaking your head up and down like Mr. "Midlife" Magoo before it's time for the close, you'd better have a little caffeine. Pack a small vial of instant coffee just in case and even a collapsible camping cup, with a few crackers, so that the caffeine will be activated gradually.

Coffee is a staple of high-achieving midlifers. They know that caffeine causes the neurons in the brain to fire faster, sharpening their wits. It is also an anti-depressant to help them through the inevitable valleys between the peaks of middle age. When taken in moderate doses, even the most sensitive stomachs don't object. If you *really* have a problem, try instant Kava, whch contains a buffering agent. Finally, it is an appetite suppressant, which will help keep you from acquiring middle-age spread. Safe and effective. Go easy on the sugar. It gives you a quick lift, but can drop your metabolism like a depth charge just as quickly.

THE SECOND HALF-HOUR

The second half-hour is to review your notes about the business, repeat the names of the people you will meet or want to mention, and visit the restroom to freshen up.

If you feel slightly tense, find a private chair, close your eyes, take a few deep breaths, exhale slowly, and imagine yourself as an employee speaking with the person you are going to meet. You might also run an ideal-job "mental movie," picturing yourself blissfully working there. These will do wonders to relax you.

Now, arrive at the reception area on time, with your resume, typed application form (unless you are a consultant), and other items in your attaché case. Greet the receptionist (an important ally), sit down, and wait. It is generally best to read your notes, the employer's newsletter, or its annual report, since newspaper and magazine articles may be distracting or upsetting.

The Magic Four Hello

When the interviewer comes out, zap him with what I call the "Magic Four Hello," which consists of four acts that occur simultaneously:

1. A smile.
2. Direct eye contact.
3. The words "Hi, I'm *(first name) (last name)*. It's a pleasure meeting you."
4. A firm but gentle handshake.

Practice makes perfect in coordinating these four elements. Aside from making the "Magic Four" flow naturally, a proper handshake is often the hardest to master.

Enthusiasm in the handshake properly sets the tempo for the interview. I would estimate that approximately one-third of the general public have a dead flounder dangling at the end of their wrist. Another third have a live shark there. By the time they reach midlife, they've become so accustomed to themselves that they don't even realize this occupational disability exists. And then there are those who hold the interviewer's outstretched hand with both of their palms, as if greeting a dear old friend. This type of effusiveness is inappropriate at a first meeting and is likely to seem artificial. Your best bet is simply to practice shaking hands with a friend who will give you honest criticism. You'll quickly be cured.

From the moment the conversation starts, avoid condescending, dusty, tired phrases like:

"At my age . . ."
"Back in the days when . . ."
"Back then . . ."
"I can't . . ."
"In the (good) old days . . ."
"It used to be that . . ."
"I remember when . . ."
"Listen, son . . ."
"Nowadays . . ."
"Old timers like me . . ."
". . . over the hill." (*Ooh!* I *hate* that one!)
"Physical exertion . . ."
"The girls in the office . . ."
". . . up in years."
"Way back when . . ."
"We used to . . ."
"When I was younger . . ."
"When I was your age . . ."
"When you get to be my age . . ."
"Years ago . . ."

Avoid the impulse to say anything negative about a former employer, boss, or colleague, no matter how bad they may have been. It will only hurt you. And also avoid the equally common impulse to put yourself down. It does not make you seem modest, but instead seems awkward, unprofessional, or even pathetic. If you're relaxed, you'll feel self-confident, which is the initial step in projecting competence—and even power.

As Herb Cohen, author of *You Can Negotiate Anything*, correctly points out:

> Power is based upon perception—if you think you've got it then you've got it. If you think you don't have it, even if you've got it, then you don't have it.[10]

You can be calm, straightforward, and unpretentious, yet still project that you've got it.

When you enter the office, admire something like a company award, trophy, art object, or item of furniture. Stay away from family pictures, clothing, and other personal things that can engender latent feelings of hostility. This starts the interviewer talking (and you listening). If possible, sit on your favored side (usually your right, interviewer's left), or sit where the interviewer will be on this side of you. Your ability to control the interview will be greatly enhanced.

Justice Richardson also had some advice about the most effective way to persuade a judge or panel of judges. He said:

> To the extent you can, keep it simple. If you can throw back to a judge his own language, his own reasoning and rationale, I think that's very effective. Judges have pride: They hope they haven't made a mistake before, and if they have, they don't like to confess it or have it pointed out.[11]

The word for this is rapport, and it can be the key to your being hired as either an employee or consultant. But now, let's take it a step further, using a specific technique:

Look the interviewer in the eye. Watch the interviewer's body language, facial expressions, eye movements, rate of speech, tone of voice, and rate of breathing. Then mirror it as much as possible, without being obvious about it. If he moves forward, you move forward. If he talks fast, you talk fast. If he uses his hands, you use your hands (hopefully not in self-defense). If he stands up, you stand up. It's known as "pacing," and is *essential* to the Nose-to-Nose Close.

In their popular book, *How to Read a Person Like a Book,* Gerard Nierenberg and Henry Calero point out:

> Feedback plays a major role in the full communication process, and gesture-clusters are an important feedback. They indicate from moment to moment and movement to movement exactly how individuals . . . are reacting nonverbally . . . We can term this *thinking through to the subconscious.*[12]

Whether you call it pacing, alignment, identification, empathy, or anything else, doesn't matter. What *does* is that at midlife you are likely to encounter an interviewer from a different generation. This means a different vocabulary, set of gestures, value system, and life-style. While it's not very likely that your interviewer is going to be a "punk-rocker," you must modify and adapt these techniques to suit your own style. The closer you come to being the same, the greater your chances of being hired. As I discussed in *How to Turn an Interview into a Job:*

> We like people who are like ourselves.[13]

It governs almost every decision we make about others, including voting, the selection of spouses and friends, television and radio choices, product purchases, and *hiring!*

You don't just want to pace, or you'll Mr. "Midlife" Magoo yourself out of the office with a *friend,* but not a *job!* You want to pace first, so you've magnetized the interviewer. Then you want to "lead" (or steer) him imperceptibly, but irresistibly, into extending the offer.

In the personnel placement bible, *Closing on Objections,* Paul Hawkinson reveals the atmosphere you can create:

No need to be stuffy, but you must immediately establish yourself as the professional. Keep small talk to a minimum and get right down to the purpose of the interview. Remember, the chummier the conversation becomes, the more difficult it is to maintain control.[14]

Listening and questioning properly *is* the Nose-to-Nose Close. Let's assume you've been sitting in the office for about five minutes, just looking like your interviewer, listening and checking everything out. You've probably been answering too. Now, you start to question. Let's read the way Paul instructs the placement professionals:

Constant questioning can be grating, and if overused, can work against you. No one wants to feel that they are on the receiving end of the prosecutor's interrogatory and questions must be used sparingly to be really effective. But they are necessary because selling is the art of asking the right questions to get the minor yes's that allow you to lead . . . to the major decision and the major yes. The final placement is nothing more than the sum total of all your yes's throughout the process. Your job, then, is to nurse the process along . . .[15]

This is done through the use of "tie-downs" in questions designed to elicit an affirmative response. Here are the more common ones:

Aren't I/you/we/they?
Can't I/he/she/you/we/they/it?
Couldn't I/he/she/you/we/they/it?
Doesn't he/she/it?
Don't I/you/we/they?
Don't you agree?
Hasn't he/she/it?
Haven't I/you/we/they?
Isn't he/she/it?

Isn't that right?
Shouldn't I/he/she/you/we/they/it?
Wasn't I/he/she/it?
Weren't you/we/they?
Won't I/he/she/you/we/they/it?
Wouldn't I/he/she/you/we/they/it?

There are four types of tie-downs, and your dialogue should vary them so that you won't appear overbearing or as though you had just arrived from the planet Midlife. If you're cookin', the interviewer will respond by agreeing with you—a minor yes.

1. The Standard Tie-down

These are used at the end of a question:

"My qualifications appear to fit the position you have open, *don't they?*"
"Company X really has a lot to offer someone with my experience, *doesn't it?*"
"It looks like we'll be able to eliminate the problem, *don't you agree?*"

2. The Inverted Tie-down

These are used at the beginning of a question:

"*Isn't it* an excellent position for someone with my background?"
"*Don't you* think we'll be working together well?"
"*Wouldn't you* like to see how I can be of assistance?"

3. The Internal Tie-down

These are used in the middle of a compound question:

"Since the entire data processing staff agrees, *shouldn't we* discuss when I can start work?"

"When the budget is approved, *won't it* expedite production to have someone who knows the project?"

"Now that we've had the opportunity to meet, *wouldn't it* be great to work together?"

4. The Tag-on Tie-down

These are used after a statement of fact. A slight pause before using the tie-down is sometimes very effective.

"My contribution to Company X will be significant, *won't it?*"

"You've really spent a lot of time and money looking for the right person, *haven't you?*"

"This problem can be corrected easily, *can't it?*"

The optimum way to learn the tie-down questioning technique is to write down as many of the four types as you think you can use during the interview. Then read them into a tape recorder and play them back once or twice a day—every day—to implant them in your subconscious. They'll pop out automatically when you need them.

After about a week of this exercise, you'll become quite articulate at the use of tie-downs. Then, practice starting out the dialogue with general questions like:

"Company X has a good reputation, *doesn't it?*"

then narrow them down to questions like:

"*Wouldn't it* be interesting to work for a supervisor like that?"

and finally:

"Shouldn't I give notice?"

Then, after about 45 minutes to an hour of interviewing, you'll be on your way. When you think the timing is right, lean slightly forward in your chair, look the interviewer in the eye (Nose-to-Nose style), and say in a declarative tone of voice something like:

> "My background fits this position well."
> "We have a good match here."
> "This looks like a long-term situation."
> "I'm excited about the position."
> "Everything looks good."

That's pacing and leading. That's using tie-downs to tie up. And that's the Nose-to-Nose Close.

Remember: Overuse of questions will make you sound like you're an applicant for a job as a game show host; if you use them sparingly you'll be effective.

Stand up, and follow through with the Magic Four Goodbye:

1. A smile.
2. Direct eye contact.
3. The words, "It sounds like a great opportunity . . . I look forward to hearing from you."
4. A firm but gentle handshake.

Then leave *without* asking for the job. Is there any doubt as to why you're there? Besides, it is too easy for those age-old insecurities to surface when your livelihood and ego are on the line.

Salary should not be discussed at this point. It is almost impossible to do so objectively, particularly if you are re-entering the job market and have no frame of reference. That is why leaving it off the fail-safe resume and writing

"OPEN" in that little rectangle on the application form will drive it up measurably.

You are in a stronger position to discuss money if the employer has already committed himself by offering you the job.

Negotiating a salary is similar to negotiating a loan: the more you appear to need it, the less likely you are to receive it.

Let the two precepts of the art of negotiating work for you: *the one who does the most talking ends up giving away the store;* and *the less you sweat, the more you get.*

Contemplate . . . let the interviewer negotiate . . . against himself. The question of whether you should ever disclose your present salary is something that you will have to decide for yourself. Salary is easy to verify by requiring proof from you (check stubs, tax returns, etc.) or contacting your last or present employer (a customary ritual). Curiously enough, the higher the position, the less likely it is that anyone will check. If you are re-entering the job market, checking is also extremely unlikely.

As a midlifer changing jobs, you have the opportunity to be creative when asked about salary. State the amount you will receive after your next review and your chances of receiving an increase ("With my forthcoming raise, my salary is _____."). Overtime possibilities should also not be overlooked, since the wages are significantly higher than those paid for straight time. What about probable bonuses? Consider pay in lieu of vacation if that is available, since your new employer probably will not allow you a vacation in your first year. If you are consulting, vacation is synonymous with "out of work," and we're not going to let *that* happen. I am *not* recommending that you falsify any information. I *am* recommending that you be aware of the hidden amounts that really add up. These are worth nothing if you don't include them, and 120 percent or more if you do. (The amount of the actual salary, plus the percentage of the increase you receive.)

Try to resist the compulsion to make yourself more desirable by negotiating away your livelihood. This is a common trap for midlifers, since they often don't realize how inflation has affected compensation. When coupled with their low self-image, it sells them short every time. If you are too cheap, the employer is psychologically inclined to think less of your talents.

Your past salary is nobody else's business, and asking about it borders on invasion of privacy. It is totally irrelevant to assessing your value in another job. Your salary requirements are also irrelevant, since the issue is whether you will accept the offer which hasn't even been extended!

These are the games employers play, and if you understand where *you* want to be, you'll know how to turn the tables on them. I didn't say not to *trust* them. Just be the one to cut the cards!

One more caution to women who are re-entering the job market: There is a tendency to sound too "domestic" in the interview, since your most recent experience is outside the world of business. Your interviewer's is inside, so keep the discussion as professional as possible.

Use the Nose-to-Nose Close from beginning to end, and you'll be hired before you can say "Midlife!"

CHAPTER 9

Networking Not Working? Get Working!

"Networking" is a mysterious-sounding word in the computer-age business world. When you first looked for a job, your elders may have told you "it's not what you know, it's who you know." Then, as you grew up, it was known as being "well-connected." Nothing has changed, except that the jobseeking sources have become better.

In *Office Politics,* Marilyn Moats Kennedy notes:

> The older worker needs to keep his or her contacts both within and outside of the organization. Unless he or she does this, the sense of job insecurity—especially in those organizations that pride themselves on being youthful—will be overwhelming. Any worker over 40 who finds himself or herself suddenly reporting to a boss 5 to 10 years younger will be glad to have kept up with his or her contacts. Then if the older worker decides, for whatever reason, that he or she has had enough of the situation, the possibilities to move without the humiliation of going through personnel, are far greater.[16]

Actually, "networking" really says it all—it's a "net" to keep you "working." You can cast it in a number of ways. Here they are in order of effectiveness:

1. Personal Contacts

The best way to look for a job is the most obvious: acquaintances, including business associates, former supervisors and co-workers, and friends. There are two ways their assistance should be sought:

Notifying you about opportunities. Their motivation to assist is best utilized by asking them to be your eyes and ears. Helping you enhances their own self-esteem. They often delight in letting you know inside information or leads that they learned about through personal observation. You should *gently* let them know if they are furnishing information on jobs that you don't want. Be grateful for any assistance, no matter how ridiculous, or you may lose more than a resource and a reference—you may lose someone who really cares during the best years of your life.

Presenting your background. Since they are your acquaintances, they will be working for you with the best intentions. Therefore, copies of your fail-safe resume and other background information should be given to them. Retype the resume, deleting anything you feel is too personal but giving them as much data as you can.

While personal contacts are a limited resource, they are only limited by your willingness to "cold-call" (the way a recruiter obtains job orders). As the intelligence-gathering phone call in Chapter 8 should convince you, a complete stranger can become a friend on the telephone in a matter of minutes. In fact, the telephone offers the opportunity to appeal to almost anyone, since all of the prejudices that relate to age, medical condition, and physical handicap are eliminated. If you loved the old radio soap operas and serials, and wonder why the television versions are no longer around, there's your answer. The use of imagination was the key to reaching the widest audience. Most midlifers remember the days of "blind dates." If you're

one of them, you'll need no further convincing about Ma
Bell's myopia.

The cold-call of today is often the reference of tomorrow, so you should look at the relationship as strictly business, intending to reciprocate. Until you're situated, try to
finesse around personal meetings with new acquaintances,
unless there's really a job opening. They can neutralize the
powerful telephone advantage and waste too much mid-
time.

Everybody is a "closet applicant" for the right job, so there
is a natural identification with someone seeking employment. A short note with the fail-safe resume enclosed will
restate your contact information, background, and appre-
ciation.

You might also check with your national or state trade
association about upcoming meetings or seminars in the
field of your choice. These usually take place at local hotels
or convention centers. If you are consulting, bring background information and business cards to leave on a table.
This will probably also get you tired before it gets you
hired, but at least it will keep you away from meeting those
valuable telephone contacts too early.

2. Forty-Plus Clubs

Unfortunately, to many employers, Forty-Plus is considered an outplacement service for a senior citizens center. You could spend your time well beyond midlife trying
to change this, so use its valuable resources quietly. Once
the contact is made, it's not necessary to walk around like
a sandwich man for Forty-Plus.

Forty-Plus Clubs are non-profit organizations located in
ten major cities. While each is autonomous, the requirements to join are the same: Over 40 years of age, and a
salary of over $25,000 per year on the last job. Business
references are checked. A few of the clubs still use a

screening committee to determine whether the applicant can be assisted, and whether he will volunteer two and a half days per week on club activities. The contribution is $250 and $3 per week.

Forty-Plus can be either terrific or terrible, depending upon your willingness to contribute and use its resources. The facilities include many (very busy) telephone lines staffed by members, phone booths where applicants can speak with employers in complete privacy, and employer interviewing offices. Newspapers; business directories; lists of employment agencies, executive recruiters, and temporary services; and job order books (constantly updated by those volunteers working the desks) make the offices a virtual gold mine of opportunity. More than 1,000 job orders are in the books alone (coded so employers will not be inundated with funny phone calls or worse).

Then there is the *Executive Manpower Directory* containing indexed, summarized backgrounds of members. In spite of its name, approximately 20 percent of the applicants are women. These are sent to around 7,500 employers. Not bad for $250 down and $3 per week!

New members are taken through an intensive "initiation ceremony" that is designed to focus them in the areas where their backgrounds can be best utilized. Then, techniques for resume writing, interviewing, and other skills are reviewed. The value of the advice will vary with the talents of the person helping you. You may find somebody who is really capable, but usually the people giving advice are unemployed themselves. See what you can learn and keep moving. You've got to get on with your midlife.

Forty-Plus Clubs can be located by simply calling directory assistance in the major metropolitan areas they serve.

Other volunteer job-finding clubs exist throughout the country, ranging from neighbors discussing local openings while jogging to highly structured sections of national professional and trade associations. If you are interested in contacting them, the primary library reference is *The Encyclopedia of Associations,* edited by Denise Akey.

For additional leads, you might let your state unemployment office know. You can either register or place a notice on the bulletin board for other jobseekers to call you. This is not the place to find a job (or boost your midlife morale), so don't waste much time there. The statistics on people who are hired through them are strictly for taxpayer consumption.

3. Employment Agencies (Employment Services, Personnel Agencies, Personnel Services, etc.)

If you are re-entering the job market, your "net" will not be "working" fully without at least six employment agencies assisting you. The counselors (consultants) make placements by separating fact from fiction, so don't expect a lot of aging assuaging. If you use the techniques we have discussed, they will have the incentive to push the buttons with employers to get you an interview. Then, it's nose-to-nose—just yours and the interviewer's.

I experienced the great feeling that motivates people in the placement industry 20 years ago, and it is still the most exciting part of my professional life. Today, there are computerized placement networks that give private agencies the ability to access hundreds of thousands of job openings and backgrounds of applicants, residing in a single zip code or anywhere in the entire country. The matching of desires, skills, and locations has completely revolutionized the prescreening process, and you belong in the free data bases. It's like a lifetime annuity. When you see a terminal on a counselor's desk, ask for a demonstration. It will amaze you.

The great strength of employment agencies is their "street sense" and flexibility to serve applicants and employers. While we will discuss temporary services in Chapter 10, many permanent agencies also have this capability, expanding the options for both parties.

If you have been away from the job market for a while, you will also be pleasantly surprised to learn that most fees are now paid by employers. This makes you a "candidate," not an "applicant" in placement vocabulary. Sounds better already!

The strategy is slightly different if you are still employed:

a. Only *one counselor* from each agency can call you at the office;
b. Everything must be *mailed to your home;* and
c. *Discretion must be used* by the agency to protect your current job.

You can also request use of your home phone number, since the answering device (discussed in Chapter 6) will always be ready.

There is a saying in the agency business:

If you don't have a "send-out" (personal interview), you won't have a placement.

Therefore, don't be too rigid about your ideal job or scheduling. If you are, you'll find yourself quietly removed from the agency's "send-out sheets."

The "third party testimonial," even by someone who stands to gain from your placement, makes the difference. On a daily basis, we see cases where an employer has received a resume directly, or even *interviewed* a midlife applicant, but nothing happened. Then along comes the right counselor, and the magic begins. A slight resume change, a word here and there in the interview, a tip about what the employer *really* wants (not just what he says), etc.

The best way to select an agency is by favorable reputation:

Good name in man and woman is the immediate jewel of their souls.

Too many midlifers forget these seventeenth century words from *Othello,* and choose career advisors by convenience, family relationship, personal friendship, number of advertisements, or other non-professional criteria. Since over 90 percent of the placement process is conducted by telephone and mail communication, this is a serious mistake.

A good reputation is the synthesis of understanding the needs of applicants and employers, and representing each ethically and professionally. Ask around—you'll hear the same good names mentioned over and over. There's a reason.

If you have been avoiding employment agencies because their reputation used to be less than sterling, I recommend that you take another look. Be prepared for an interview.

Employment agencies are found in almost all regions and are in the Yellow Pages listings under "Employment Agencies," "Employment-Permanent," "Personnel Agencies," or similar headings.

4. Executive Recruiters (Professional/Management/ Technical Recruiters, Executive/Professional/ Management/Technical Search Firms, Executive/ Professional/Management/Technical Consultants, "Headhunters," etc.)

Every profession has its aristocracy; in law it's those corporate Beverly Hills three-piecers (oops!); in medicine it's the brain surgeons; in placement it's the executive recruiters. How sweet it is . . . all those Fortune 500's just *itching* to drop their "procurement budgets" on them to "survey," "conduct," "search," "identify," "analyze," "qualify," and "refer"!

With the increasing professionalism of the placement industry, employer-paid fees, and more sophisticated applicants, most executive recruiters and employment agencies perform exactly the same function, exactly the same way. Approximately 5 percent are employer-retained, and the rest operate on a nonexclusive contingency fee basis. The fees are generally based upon a percentage of the projected annual starting salary of the applicant. They average around $8,000.

These organizations tend to be owned by management and sales-oriented individuals from almost every industry. They thrive on the chase (identification) and kill (placement). They are quick of flight and have a positive attitude, sensitive faculties, and a keen sense of timing.

Several of the larger national recruiting organizations are owned by major corporations, and most have developed a franchise system. Virtually all the recruiters and office managers are compensated based upon the placement fees received or "cash in." Some (particularly the personnel management refugees from industry) use big words. Most know the ropes and the rules. If you use the techniques in this book, they'll all be eager to present you for suitable openings.

Recruiters are successful because they know where the action is in the employment market. They know employers from the inside, where midlife politics and age discrimination hide. They know who has exciting products on the boards, and who is about to lose key employees. They know who promotes from within and who stifles creativity. They know who pays well and who has high turnover. They know for the same reason you will know—they listen.

Executive recruiters tend to cluster in major cities and can be found in Yellow Pages listings under "Executive Recruiting Consultants," "Management Consultants," "Personnel Consultants," "Employment Agencies," or variations of these headings.

5. Job Clearinghouses (Employment Clearinghouses, Job/Employment Listing Services, Job/Employment Directory Services, Job/Employment Finding Services, Job/Employment Banks, Job/Employment Registries, Job/Employment "Hotline" Operators, etc.)

Job clearinghouses vary widely in the services they provide. Their primary competitor is the help-wanted section of the newspaper. Some job listing services actually "cold-call" employers to obtain job orders, while others simply rerun information from traditional sources (civil service bulletins, alumni office postings, newspaper advertisements, etc.). These are only as good as the leads published in their newsletter or computer printout. Since invariably a clearinghouse is a secondary source, you might find that many of the positions are no longer available. You probably won't find these listed in the Yellow Pages under any conventional headings.

Next we move into the area of marginal assistance, but you should at least be aware of what's out there.

6. Letter-writing Services (Career Planning Centers, etc.)

Letter-writing services prepare a form letter for the applicant and send it to potential employers. Around 90 percent of their "clients" are midlifers. Sometimes it is just an inquiry letter, other times it includes a resume prepared by the service. Word processors or offset printing are used. The list is usually computerized, and is obtained

from the Yellow Pages, trade directories, college placement guides, chamber of commerce rosters, and compila-
tions found in the business section of any bookstore or
library. Therefore, they aim at a mass-market moving target of openings.

This is what is known in the placement business as
"throwing enough resumes against the wall, and hoping
some of them stick." It's a masochistic midlife when you
do it that way. Personnel interviewers can spot commercially prepared letters and resumes even before the envelope is opened. The typeface, stationery, and metered
postage from the same city are obvious, and the probability of the envelope even being opened is remote. You
should feel flattered if you rate a rejection letter.

When I was a personnel staffer, we had a special "in
basket" for these. "In" was short for "indefinitely." This
was so we could comply with the record-retention laws.

So think twice when somebody urges you to use a letter-
writing service.

7. Resume Services:

It is amazing how many otherwise intelligent people go to
a resume service. In some cases, the resume is part of a
letter-writing campaign, in others it is just the resume.
Either way, it's the sign of a professional applicant who
lacks the greatest gift of midlife: common sense.

It is axiomatic among those who are hiring:

The more show in the resume, the less glow in the applicant.

Right or wrong, you're subject to that axiom.

One or more fail-safe resumes can be typeset and run
by any competent printer. Within the parameters discussed in Chapter 6, you can even be *slightly* creative. Let

your resume show that you went through the mental process of taking your adult experience and distilling it down to one concise, carefully worded, grammatically correct, properly spelled portrait suitable for framing. Fight your way through it, word by word. Make every word count.

You'll interview far better once you've finished the resume yourself. All they know is what you show.

8. Career Consultants (Career Counselors, Career Advisors, Guidance Counselors, etc.)

Ah, midman's inhumanity to midman (and midwoman)!

It's not unusual to be charged $20,000 for a slick battery of vocational guidance tests that show you should be doing anything but what you've done, and where you've done it. Then, of course, it's the old form letter, "experience summary" (12-page resume) routine. Postage included, of course.

The first clue is the display ad in the newspaper disclaiming that they will find you a job. The second is the high-rent location. The third is the foxy receptionist. Some states don't even permit this type of service.

There are some legitimate career consultants out there, but check personal and business references carefully.

9. Psychological Testing Services

The most comical job I ever had was working part-time for a licensed clinical psychologist who administered pre-employment tests to applicants. He was a brilliant fellow but couldn't write very well. My job was to take his notes from all the vocational aptitude and projective tests administered the day before and write intelligible evaluations to submit to the employer.

Another associate in the office was present while the

tests were being administered. He would write down how the psychologist appeared to be feeling. I would work up the evaluations from the notes and scores, and then independently write down my opinion of how the psychologist felt. We did a comparison every day for the entire summer, and I was never wrong. Unfortunately, I couldn't tell you a *thing* about the applicants.

Psychological testing does have some validity to employers *if* the test scores have been "validated" to correlate to success in a specific job. But you are considering all of the options now, and there are too many variables to make the results useful. The danger is that you will be discouraged from pursuing opportunities because of some abstract notion of what attributes are required for certain occupations.

All the self-analysis you need has occurred by midlife, and if you followed the exercises in Chapter 3, you have organized your experience into an accurate guide.

10. Image Consultants (Personal Agents, Business Managers, etc.)

It is difficult to generalize in this area, since these folks will do everything from teaching you how to dress to propping you up during the interview.

There is an infinite amount of information out there on packaging yourself for sale to a prospective employer. Much of it is contradictory and therefore the professional objectivity of a trained consultant can be valuable.

You can obtain advice on a fixed-fee basis from image consultants, either in group sessions or individually. However, beware of those who try to sell you goods or additional services. Vanity is a billion-dollar business, and midlifers in a youth-oriented world are steady customers.

A good source for additional network contacts is *The National Job Finding Guide* by Heinz Ulrich and J. Robert

Connor. It is available in the reference section of most libraries.

So there you have it. Networking really isn't so mysterious after all. Finding a job will always be something you must do for yourself. The linkage of professional contacts you make can help you enjoy your midyears beyond anything you ever imagined.

Happy casting!

CHAPTER 10

Part-Time Employment, Job Sharing and Temporary Assignments

As you can see from the chapter heading, there really *are* a number of ways to free yourself from a 9-to-5 routine. If you are not working, they are midlife keys for re-entry into the job market. Since they are unconventional, you may need to explain them to an employer, so I will give you an overview of each and the technique for doing so.

1. Part-Time Employment

In the classic part-time arrangement, you simply work less than 40 hours. Federal law doesn't distinguish categories of employees, so all payroll deductions are simply reduced on a pro rata basis. Since states vary widely in eligibility for mandatory programs, (unemployment and disability insurance, etc.), be sure to check with your local labor department. Depending upon the employer, eligibility for group life and health insurance, vacation and holiday pay, and everything else down to blood donations may be foreclosed. Your newly acquired negotiating skill may change this though.

During my last year of night law school (paid for by my employer), I was working as a personnel manager for a division of a major corporation. I was feeling the strain of so many who try to keep one foot on a secure job, while stretching the other to reach that next step to fame and fortune. I had to make a choice, because the last year of law school is the toughest, and then there's the greatest hurdle of all—the bar examination.

I was on a tightrope juggling act, and swaying. Remembering that advice about not looking down, I marched right into my boss's office. Waiting would have turned the strain into a spasm. Here's the script:

Jeff: Hi, Frank.

Frank: Hi, Jeff. What's the latest on the director of marketing opening?

Jeff: I've got three recruiters working on it. Do you want to blow the procurement budget by running an ad?

Frank: No, I don't think so. I enjoy doing the job too much, and we're saving a fortune.

Jeff: OK. I'll see if I can find a few more headhunters to work on the assignment.

Frank: Sounds good.

Jeff: Frank, I really came in to talk about law school.

Frank: I already told you, we won't pay for your bar exam review course.

Jeff: No, I need your advice. (As a midlifer, Frank had the primordial urge to give advice. It was unfair, but I was desperate.)

Frank: Advice, counsel?

Jeff: Yes, I've got the personnel department under control, and actually could do the job half-time. It would save the division almost $15,000 in my salary alone!

Frank: What about the rest of the troops? What about
         the fancy employee handbook you prepared? I
         can't have my staff people making their own
         hours . . . the personnel manager, of *all* people!
         If the president ever found out, how could I
         explain it?

 Jeff: I can come in every morning at eight and stay
         through noon. If I need to stay around and in-
         terview an applicant or handle an emergency, I'll
         do it.

Frank: Are you asking me or telling me?

 Jeff: I'm asking you. I really appreciate your assis-
         tance, and enjoy working here. This will save us
         a lot of money, won't it? (A standard tie-down—
         see Chapter 8.)

Frank: I can certainly see that. (A minor yes—see Chap-
         ter 8.) But if we have any problems, you'd better
         be here. (Giving orders was not one of Frank's
         problems.)

 Jeff: Fair enough. How do you want to handle it?
         (Working on that primordial "advice" urge
         again.)

Frank: No announcements. Just be cool about it. We'll
         cut your salary and keep the benefits intact until
         I decide what to do with you.

The result was that I worked on a part-time basis for
about two years, and it was a "win-win" situation for both
parties. Everybody loved the arrangement. I didn't have
to look busy, watching the clock. The company received a
solid four hours a day, with an occasional cameo appear-
ance at company functions that worked out just fine. My
reasons were:

a. Retention of a valued employee;
b. Increased productivity; and
c. Reduction in cost.

Here are other reasons you can use to reduce existing hours, if you'd like to return to school, look for another job, or start your own business:

d. Delegation of duties to other employees;
e. Reduction in absenteeism;
f. Reduction in turnover;
g. Increased flexibility in scheduling; and
h. Better utilization of space.

There may be even more, so look around.

As with every team effort, communication, coordination, and a flexible outside schedule are necessary. That's why your maturity (and the absence of young children) is such an asset for this arrangement.

If you intend to work part-time for a new employer, your first step should be to adapt the Consultant Phone Call discussed in Chapter 7. One of the reasons it works so well is that it is essentially a non-threatening, benign toss of a life raft. Those who feel themselves sinking will respond. Those who don't, won't. It is the same approach you should use for your part-time marketing, starting with the Yellow Pages.

There are other advantages to an employer hiring you as a part-time employee. It is often easier to justify the small increase in budget if it is a new job rather than a replacement; it allows the hiring authority to look good because he may actually be able to *reduce* the budget if there is an existing job opening; it permits the employer to try you out without making the commitment of full-time employment; and it may provide greater flexibility in the use of human resources. These are advantages you may wish to mention in your conversation with the interviewer. The opportunities are all around you, but you must know how to use them.

2. Job Sharing

The associates in our Beverly Hills office have utilized a job sharing system for the receptionist, paralegal, and law clerk duties for over five years. In fact, the independent attorneys job-share as well. It is nothing more than a service-oriented team effort, with one or more attorneys primarily responsible. It also evens out the caseload.

In the non-professional area, two part-time employees split the regular hours. For openers, it has all of the advantages discussed with part-time employment. But this is only the beginning. Two heads really can be better than one in determining the best procedure to use, and can perform research far more effectively. In fact, twice as much knowledge, creativity, and skill is brought to bear on the same problem.

Absenteeism, a constant panic situation in office jobs, is no longer a concern. There is always at least one person who can come in early, work late, or switch shifts. In fact, it's their responsibility to figure out the coverage and enter the time accordingly. A built-in check and balance system exists by the dual arrangement. Each is automatically supervising the other.

Turnover is lessened because job-sharers are not likely to be as dependent upon the paycheck or constrained by the rigid hours of full-time work. In the repetitive jobs, "burn-out" from boredom or stress doesn't take twice as long—it's practically non-existent.

In the professional area, the lawyers are able to use their specialties to the greatest advantage. The combined years of legal experience can potentially be mobilized on any case. You can see how valuable job sharing is for law firms.

Other professions that benefit from this concept are medicine, teaching, accounting, and marriage. At midlife, the peace of mind *alone* makes the concept worthwhile.

The techniques to either convert your present job or prospect for a new one are exactly the same as with part-time employment. Be prepared to provide information, since it is a relatively new concept.

If job sharing had been customary in the early seventies, Frank could have "advised" me to do it!

A particularly good source for further information is *The Complete Guide to Job Sharing* by Patricia Lee (and others, of course).

3. Temporary Assignments

The temporary field is easily the fastest-growing segment of the placement industry. This is because it makes so much sense for both the employee and "client."

Several years ago, a representative from the EEOC was discussing an age discrimination charge with me filed against a temporary service. He was about to close the file, since there was no evidence to support the alleged discriminatory practice. His comment was, "Temporary services tend to be blind to discrimination. So do their clients."

This is because the service wants as many employees in its inventory as possible, since *availability* on short notice is imperative. Since it usually doesn't know where the person will be sent, discrimination is the *last* thing on anyone's mind! Someone who needs a helicopter to get to work, yes. Age, no. It is unquestionably the fastest way to full- or part-time employment. You can register with as many services as you like. The first caller wins the prize.

In many ways, working on "temp assignments" gives you the best of both worlds. It releases most of the pressure in the employment relationship, since the client knows if he makes your midlife too miserable, another (maybe even a *younger*) person will be there in the morning. That knowledge has a very salutary effect on even the most brutal slavedriver.

If you enjoy the visiting hours, that's another matter. In fact, "employee leasing" is nothing more than an extended temporary facelift (with a few permanent wrinkles). The more common method for extended employment is a "temp-to-perm conversion," however. If the client wants you on a long-term basis, he can simply call the service and ask for a transfer to his payroll. Many even waive the conversion fee after the assignment has lasted a specified period of time (usually 90 days). At least theoretically, the difference between what the client pays and what you cost makes the transaction worthwhile for the service. It can lose a client *and* an employee if it's too uncooperative.

The dynamics of a temporary assignment are made for the midlifer looking to get past the age barrier. When you arrive, the client won't care about your age. In fact, most are too preoccupied to even remember your name. Then, after you've become indispensable, he *really* won't care about your age!

Clerical and technical support jobs were the traditional office temporary service areas. Now, engineering, accounting, and data processing professionals are dispatched on a regular basis. Some are employees, others are consultants ("independent contractors"). Call your state labor department to find out whether anything but being on the payroll is legal. The temporary service ("job shop") may be subjecting both of you to liability for taxes, personal injury, and other items without realizing it.

A well-written book on the subject is *Working Whenever You Want* by Barbara Johnson. A few of our clients in the temporary service industry assisted (another job share!).

Although we discussed direct consulting as a way of obtaining interviews in Chapter 7, you might want to consider it as a way of life also. Some of the most unemployable elders I've ever known have been on "consulting assignments" with one or more businesses for years in executive, professional, technical, and even administrative positions. They're sheltering so much income in their own pension plans that it would be impossible for any group plan to compete. They don't worry about watching the clock, payroll withholding, or the corporate bureaucracy. Many wish they'd joined the "advice squad" long ago. You could do far worse.

Just the exploration of these alternatives alone should give you some insight into the incredible opportunities that exist in working for other people. In Chapter 12, we'll discuss how you can create your own.

CHAPTER 11

An Employment Agreement: the Midlife Bottom Line

Employment agreements are designed to objectify the employment relationship. For the midlife employee, job security is generally the bottom line. For the employer, protection against liability for breaching pre-employment promises, discrimination, and wrongful termination is becoming essential. The terms vary greatly, but the objectives for both parties don't.

By the time most of us have reached midlife, the myth of continued employment has been pretty well shattered. Over the past decade, the number of employment agreements we prepare for senior employees has increased by more than 20 percent per year. Economic uncertainty and the growing number of older people in the working population will undoubtedly continue this trend. We call them "midlife job insurance policies." Employers are surprisingly receptive to signing them, although you should not expect to get one unless the position is in middle or upper management.

There are four "P"s to consider: Person, Proper Timing, Presentation, and Policy.

1. Person

You can sit there bangin' your gums for hours in front of an interviewer who may agree with everything you say. In his mind, though, you're just a midlife malcontent. "What's wrong with exercising a little patience to avoid a charge of discrimination?," he thinks.

Employment interviewers are the last people to approach with agreements. For one thing, they are administrators, and anything that looks *different* looks *wrong*. For another, they fear that if your employment agreement is signed, armed insurrection will occur among the troops.

As Tessa Albert Warschaw observes in *Winning by Negotiation:*

> Be certain . . . that when you're talking, it's to the right people . . . The question uppermost in your mind ought to be whether the person from whom you're seeking the power to accomplish something has the power to give it to you.[17]

You want to be sure you're talking to a decision maker; not just someone who can make a recommendation, but a hiring authority. Someone who has all of the pressure of having to get the job done *yesterday*.

2. Proper Timing

If you've followed the techniques discussed throughout the book, you have undoubtedly noticed that you are on the high side of the employment seesaw. In negotiating terms, this has given you distinct leverage. Once you are hired, you run the danger of landing on the ground with a thud. That's why approximately 80 percent of all employment agreements are executed prior to an employee reporting for work. However, they are almost never successfully presented on the first interview.

If you are called back for a second interview, you will receive an offer about 60 percent of the time. Knowing this, you will be more confident. Much of the fear of the unknown has disappeared. You will be getting down to business with your future boss. The interviewer is now relegated to merely administering.

Tessa Warschaw has some advice about this also:

> Make a decision that you have a right to be there. You wouldn't be there in the first place if you didn't have the qualifications.[18]

You make your move regarding an employment agreement as soon as you're offered a job.

3. Presentation

As with any insurance selling, you really have to rehearse the sales pitch. Our offices are so sure that the correct presentation will work, that we have actually *guaranteed* that if we prepare one that is not signed, we will refund half the fee. After ten years and hundreds of agreements, there are only about fifteen cases where this was necessary. Even in those, several "P"s were missing.

The conversation leads up to your maneuver in a remarkably predictable way. It is this predictability that makes it so controllable. Now it's your turn; consider this scenario:

Supervisor: Well, I guess you've gathered that we're interested in having you come to work for us. How does it sound to you?

You: It sounds like an ideal position for me to use my experience productively.

Supervisor: We've decided to offer you the position of manager of consumer affairs, starting at $42,000. This will allow for additional increases within the rate range. Your performance will be reviewed in 90 days, and you will be eligible for a merit increase after six months. I assume you've discussed our annual review policy and company benefits with the personnel department.

You: Yes, I have. The salary sounds fine, and the opportunity is exactly what I've been seeking. Don't you think we should prepare a short agreement outlining the terms? (An inverted tie-down—see Chapter 8.)

Supervisor: We've never used them, and our corporate attorney is very conservative. We think we've got a good match here, and I'd really like to wrap this thing up.

You: I agree. I'm anxious to assist you. Why don't I either bring the agreement to you at nine tomorrow morning, or leave it with the receptionist downstairs? Then we can discuss it. Of course, it will be in a sealed envelope, marked "Confidential." I'm preparing it myself. It's really just a memorandum of understanding.

Supervisor: Well, OK. I'll speak to the vice president of administration and see if I can get approval in advance. When can you start? (A major yes—see Chapter 8.)

You: I should give my present employer two weeks' notice . . . My boss would appreciate that, since I have major responsibilities. If you like, I'll explain that you need me right away, and leave it up to him. Once he recovers from the shock, I'm sure he'll understand.

Supervisor:　It would really help me out. We've been in-undated with inquiries from customers!

You:　No problem. I've handled these successfully in the past. Why don't I take some files with me? I'm anxious to get started.

Supervisor:　Fine. Jeanne will take you to the Consumer Affairs Department, and we'll find some homework for you.

You:　Great. (Magic Four Goodbye time—see Chapter 8.) I'll leave the papers with the re-ceptionist in the morning.

Supervisor:　OK. I'll call you in the afternoon when they're approved, and you can give notice.

You will note that there was an optimistic, enthusiastic, action-oriented tenor to the conversation. No talk about being left up your life without a paddle. No talk about running to a lawyer. A mere formality.

The meeting really can go this smoothly, and you can find yourself subtly in control. Now let's shift the scenario —skip directly home. Plug in your typewriter, keep the book open, and let's go to the next step.

4. Policy

A major reason our employment agreements are signed is that they are properly *packaged*. Would *you* sign a 15-page insurance policy that was one long, fine-print, multisyl-labic-worded, compound sentence? Not a chance. How about one that used slang and bound nobody? Even less likely. Over two-thirds of the employment agreements we see fall into these categories. They also fall into the round file.

TITLE

If you entitled it "EMPLOYMENT CONTRACT" (which it is), you can bet your midlife it will be reviewed by an attorney. A recent study by the Chiquita Foundation revealed that no two attorneys peel a banana the same way. That means "delay." And that means "no sale." Ask any insurance salesperson:

The longer the wait, the less likely the sale.

SAMPLE PARAGRAPH

In consideration of *(name of employer)* ("EMPLOYER") hiring *(first name) (last name)* ("EMPLOYEE"), it is agreed as follows:

No advanced Legalese, just enough to evidence contractual intent.

SAMPLE PARAGRAPH

A gross amount of $_____ per _____ shall be paid by EMPLOYER to EMPLOYEE, less any customary and usual deductions for the performance of services in the initial position of _____. Said gross amount shall be increased by at least _____ percent per year on or before the anniversary date of EMPLOYEE. Changes in status or promotions shall be at the sole discretion of EMPLOYER.

This paragraph is usually on the first page of the agreement, so it is particularly important that it look sharp. It discusses another bottom line—money. You should leave the percentage of increase blank, since by inserting the number the supervisor will feel he has negotiated the agreement. This single device has been one of the most effective in getting the employer to sign, and really gives up nothing, since invariably a supervisor will insert an amount approximately two percentage points higher than the cost of living. Don't ask me why, but that's the phenomenon of contemplating salary, and letting the employer do the negotiating against himself. You'll recall that we discussed this in Chapter 8.

There is a temptation for midlifers to overwrite the agreement. As with the passage of time, the longer it is, the less likely that it will be signed. The benefit package will be standard. The equal employment opportunity, labor, insurance, and pension laws are there to protect you. Let them.

SAMPLE PARAGRAPH

If EMPLOYER terminates the employment of EMPLOYEE after 90 days for any reason other than a specific violation of a written policy formerly acknowledged by EMPLOYEE, _____ times the current weekly gross amount shall be immediately paid to EMPLOYEE. Said amount includes pay in lieu of notice and severance pay, but excludes any personal leave, sick leave, holiday, vacation, or other pro rata termination pay in accordance with the policy of EMPLOYER.

As with the salary increase, it will be necessary to insert the amount of severance pay. If you can ascertain what the company normally pays by a quick call to the personnel department, without revealing that you are preparing an employment agreement, do so. Then double it. Otherwise, four weeks is generally the maximum a new hire can receive.

Aside from the equal employment opportunity laws, your employment is still basically *terminable at will.* Attempting to force the employer to retain your services when you're not performing is *exactly the opposite* of the approach you should be taking. It won't take long for someone to decide you'll become a midlife morale problem.

SAMPLE PARAGRAPH

EMPLOYEE acknowledges that the internal procedures, records, lists, forms, and other proprietary information developed or obtained by EMPLOYER in the course of its business operations are confidential trade secrets, and shall remain the exclusive property of EMPLOYER. Accordingly, EMPLOYEE shall not retain, duplicate, disclose, or use any of said information, except in furtherance of the employment.

This is a great way to proclaim your professional responsibility. It simply states the existing case law at both the federal and state levels, and therefore is just a way to show good faith. It is also a way to avoid liability for "unfair competition" if you leave. Employers are notoriously paranoid about the extent of their trade secrets and by "acknowledging" this you demonstrate your concern.

This paragraph accounts for a large number of agreements being signed, and is often adopted later by employers for all employees. You're assisting already!

SAMPLE PARAGRAPH

EMPLOYEE agrees to act in an attentive, ethical, and responsible manner, and to exclusively represent EMPLOYER at all times with the utmost concern for its goals, interests, and image with employees, suppliers, customers, and members of the general public.

Known as a "best efforts" paragraph, this is standard fare in employment agreements. As you may know, the law implies that every contract contains a covenant of good faith and cooperation, regardless of its recital. However, from your standpoint it is better to include it, since it counterbalances the few items you want.

SAMPLE PARAGRAPH

If it becomes necessary for EMPLOYEE or EMPLOYER to enforce or interpret the terms of this Agreement, the matter shall be settled by binding arbitration under the auspices and in accordance with the rules of the American Arbitration Association. Judgment on the award rendered may be entered in any court of competent jurisdiction.

This paragraph is extremely important for you, since it is probable that the employer can more likely afford to litigate a dispute through the court system. It is not unusual for employees to either abandon a valid claim or wipe out their midlife savings in prosecuting or defending one. Binding arbitration is a professional, relatively painless, inexpensive, and realistic way to resolve disputes. The American Arbitration Association's rules are accepted and fair.

SAMPLE PARAGRAPH

Neither EMPLOYEE nor EMPLOYER shall disclose either the existence of this Agreement or any of its terms for the duration of the employment. If EMPLOYEE shall directly or indirectly cause such disclosure, EMPLOYER may immediately terminate the employment, as though a written policy formerly acknowledged by EMPLOYEE had been violated.

Since you are not a labor organizer, only an organized laborer, there is no danger in keeping the agreement confidential. In fact, it is one of the best marketing devices to get it signed immediately. We discussed the reasons briefly earlier in the chapter.

SAMPLE DATE AND SIGNATURE LINES

DATED: _____ _____, 19____
_____
(name of employer)
("EMPLOYER")

By: _____
(first name)   *(last name)*

Title: _____
_____
(first name)   *(last name)*
("EMPLOYEE")

Although a formal agreement has more psychological impact, a letter agreement is just as valid. Of course, nothing is valid if it's not signed, so if you believe a letter agreement will fly more readily, the following should appear after your signature:

THE ABOVE TERMS ARE HEREBY ACCEPTED.

DATED: _____ _____, 19____
_____
(name of employer)
("EMPLOYER")

By: _____
(first name)   *(last name)*

Title: _____

If you have arranged a consulting assignment, you can use the same format, changing "EMPLOYEE" to "CONSULTANT," and eliminating any reference to employment or employee benefits.

The variations on employment agreements are limited only by the number of words in English and Legalese, and it is easy for a lay person to become confused, particularly when time is of the essence. That is why I have given you one of *our* trade secrets. We began this chapter with a discussion of the four "P"s. May the *fifth* "P" for you be *Permanence!*

CHAPTER 12

Your Own Business: Nothing Like It

One of the great rewards of being a business attorney is to consult with someone about to become an entrepreneur.

The excitement, energy, and creativity that abounds when someone makes the decision to "go for it" is a thrill that can easily bring tears of joy to your eyes. I have been privileged to witness this with hundreds of clients and to watch them as their ideas were transformed into reality. My wife, Bev, started her own successful retail business with a partner at midlife, so I see free enterprise in action on a daily (and nightly) basis.

As the years have passed, it has become relatively easy to isolate the factors that make the difference between success and failure in doing your own thing. In order of importance, they are motivation, experience, and money.

1. Motivation

This means making the decision and emotionally living or dying by it. The famous sports figure Tommy Lasorda captured the feeling when he said:

Managing the world champion baseball team has given me some insight about what motivates people. It's not just the glory and the money as much as the burning desire to be number one—to be part of a winning team. I'm used to working with winners. They're competitive, disciplined and determined to be the best.

There's no doubt about it: If you don't step up to the plate, you can't hit a home run. Deep down in your soul, you must feel, "Get outa my way—I'm comin' through!" Only then do you have the belief in yourself and the stamina to go through or around all of the roadblocks.

Once you've made the commitment, you'll notice the usual changes: Staying awake at night, avoiding your family responsibilities, being impatient with others, writing reminders to yourself, chasing after business leads, looking at office space, inquiring about printing and phone costs, engaging in other compulsive behavior, and feeling a gnawing in the pit of your stomach are the early signs. You're not sick, you're just in love—with an idea.

One of the first things our clients notice is that they're working much longer hours, much harder, and for much less money than they ever did on a job. But they're also getting much greater satisfaction. This is the American free enterprise spirit alive and well.

It's great to be your own boss. Nobody likes to be told what to do. That's why they call it "work." That's why they pay you to do it. If you're an entrepreneur at heart, you probably *hate* it.

2. Experience

There's that middle-age word again.

Most people would agree that the practice of law or medicine requires a high degree of knowledge and skill. However, a practicing lawyer or doctor spends less than

10 percent of professional time in anything that requires independent judgment. Even in these technical disciplines, over 90 percent is common sense and general knowledge. The less skilled the occupation, the lower the percentage of independent judgment required. That is the reason automation continues to displace millions of midlifers every year.

Business is common sense, and business understanding is highly transferable. In fact, many employers won't hire executives from their own industry. They would rather have new ideas than merely an understanding of their products. They would rather train than attempt to retrain.

3. Money:

Contrary to popular belief, capital is really far less important than motivation and experience. I started our law practice with a $25 gift. While I don't recommend this, it can be done. So much depends upon the type of business, that it is difficult to generalize. Accountants recommend that you plan to sustain a loss for the first year, and to expect no income for at least three years. Hunger is a great incentive. Loan repayment is not. If you don't have it, don't spend it.

If you are still in doubt about what you'd like to do with your midlife, reviewing the completed job forms from Chapter 3 should give you the direction. The past jobs show what you've done and the ideal job bridges to what you'd like to do. If you would like to brainstorm, prepare a form like the one shown listing the experience as it relates to a business that looks appealing. Be realistic.

EXPERIENCE	BUSINESS
1.	a.
	b.
	c.
2.	a.
	b.
	c.
3.	a.
	b.
	c.
4.	a.
	b.
	c.
5.	a.
	b.
	c.
6.	a.
	b.
	c.

There are an endless number of businesses you can start on your own, with new ones being added every day. Any list I could give you would be too confining. Public libraries are filled with this information, though, so you might find yourself still completing lists when the lights flicker at closing time.

Before we leave this phase, I should warn you about an insidious midlife phenomenon I call "negative rush." This was observed particularly well by Michael Korda in his bestseller, *Success!:*

> ... [M]any of us feel profoundly and unconsciously that "the higher you climb, the harder you fall," and solve the problem by not climbing at all ... The methods by which people assure their own failure are subtle, devious and complex, so much so that you may be unable to see just how you have done it.[19]

It's a four-step process, starting with an idea. Let's watch how it works:

Idea:	You think, "I'll become a real estate agent."
Visualization:	You see yourself selling a property.
Negative Rush:	You think, "But the examination is so difficult. I'll never pass."
Conclusion:	You think, "Why bother?"

Of course, you want to be realistic. But here is an example of how you decided "I can't" ("Why bother?") before any research, let alone any attempt, occurred. We naturally shift from risk to security as we get older, but sometimes we get too close to the grave. Too many of us merely endure our precious midlife imprisoned by our own low self-esteem.

Even changing your attitude won't make you successful. *Doing* something for yourself will.

As Brian Wood, publisher of *Entrepreneur Magazine*, notes:

> Every profitable business started as a dream carried by an entrepreneur who saw a need and filled it. Through a combination of hard work, proper planning, and giving the public what it wants, those tiny ideas become real giants.[20]

Once you've identified what you want to do, we're ready to go through the paces of starting your own business.

1. Buying an Existing Business

While most midlifers think about starting a new business first, you shouldn't overlook the advantages to buying an existing business:

a. *Fewer mistakes.*   One of the great advantages of midlife is that you've already learned from your mistakes along the way. When you start your own business, it's like growing up all over again. With an existing business, the time, expense and discouragement can be minimized.

b. *Less work.*   The business is already in place, so the initial decisions about location, equipment, forms, advertising, pricing, and many other items have been made.

c. *Access to information.*   The seller may be willing to share his experience with you. It is common for the purchase agreement to include a specific period of time for you to work together during the transition.

d. *Established customers.*   Almost every business develops a residual value just by being there. This is known as "blue sky" because it is hard to quantify, but it is an asset that really makes a difference.

e. *Dependable suppliers.*   Developing favorable relationships with those who provide goods and services is a time-consuming, trial-and-error activity. A going business has already done it.

f. *Existing employees.*   While you might not want to keep the same staff, continuity is more likely when it remains.

The longer you are there, the less important this becomes.

g. *Favorable price.* There are often legitimate personal reasons for a seller to reduce the price below the market value. Once someone decides to sell, it's like a psychological rollercoaster going downhill. In fact, the feelings are exactly the opposite of the buyer's. This is why negotiating is so difficult for both parties, but the less you telegraph your enthusiasm, the lower the price.

As with jobseeking, the telephone is your best friend when looking for a business to buy. Just pick up the Yellow Pages and look under the headings that interest you. Call and ask for the *owner* without stating your reason. If you've got the cash, he'll probably have the time. Should you receive a negative response, be *sure* to leave your name and phone number. Forty percent of the time, you'll be called back within two weeks by an interested owner. A low price could just mean mismanagement or a desire to leave the business. A high price could be just a negotiating "opener." In either case, don't let the initial amount frighten you.

Just arrange for a personal visit. The Yellow Pages also has a heading entitled "Business Brokers." These folks are constantly soliciting sellers, and since they are paid only if there is a sale, they are a great source of free information. Business associations, chambers of commerce, and similar organizations can provide valuable leads too.

2. Type of Organization

There are really only three types: sole proprietorship, partnership, and corporation.

If you start as a sole proprietor and use any name other than your own, it will probably be necessary for you to file a "fictitious business name statement" with the city or county clerk. Then, it usually must be published in a local newspaper, so that if someone has a claim against the business, they can catch up with you. But don't be misled by the word "fictitious." There is nothing illegal about it. A "dba" ("doing business as . . .") is the same thing.

In fact and in law, a partnership is the same: two or more people engaged in a common enterprise, which each owns equally. A formal agreement is not essential but should be used so that there is no misunderstanding from the very beginning. If one does arise, at least a vehicle to resolve it will exist.

A partnership is merely an *aggregate* of its individual members. Sometimes, people starting a business assume that a fictitious business name filing, business license, or partnership tax return alters this status. They don't. As to third persons dealing with the partnership, each partner may be considered *his brother's keeper* and held liable for the acts of every other partner in the course of their business.

It is this attribute of unlimited *joint and several liability* that makes a partnership an extremely precarious and fragile form of business organization, and accounts for the fact that many partnerships either dissolve entirely or are converted into corporations. Those that remain consist largely of family-owned businesses.

A corporation is a legal entity that exists pursuant to a grant or *franchise* from the state. It is a *person* under the law and, if properly formed and maintained, has an existence separate and distinct from its owner(s).

A brief review of your local Yellow Pages will reveal that almost all successful businesses are incorporated. If the words "Inc.," "Corp.," or "Ltd." don't appear, it is probably just a fictitious business name filed by a corporation.

The *framework* of a corporation includes:

ARTICLES OF INCORPORATION

Sometimes referred to as the *charter*, the filed articles represent a *license* from the state to transact business and define the nature and extent of the privilege. Until suspended, revoked, dissolved, or otherwise terminated, the license remains valid.

BY-LAWS

By-laws are the *rules and regulations* that provide the operating system for internal corporate functioning. In addition, all corporations are required to maintain certain records, including *minutes* of board of directors and shareholder meetings, *books of account,* and a *share register.*

The *functions* within a corporation include:

SHAREHOLDERS

Shareholders are the *owners* of the corporation, and generally have the right to vote for directors. Distributions of profit are often in the form of *dividends* in proportion to share ownership.

DIRECTORS

Collectively, the board of directors is vested with overall management and control of the corporation. Directors are the corporate trustees or *fiduciaries,* and are responsible for making the policy decisions that enable it to function.

OFFICERS

The president, vice president, secretary, and treasurer are the corporate officers and executives selected by the board. They are so named because they *execute* its policies in furtherance of business operations. Under many state laws, a *single individual* can perform all of these functions. As an officer, you become an employee, and are paid a salary just as if you worked for a stranger.

Due to its *separate legal status,* a corporation enjoys many advantages found in no other type of business organization. Among them are:

a. *Limited liability* of the owners;
b. *Name protection* (assuming you don't use a fictitious name);
c. Ability to *transfer ownership interest;*
d. *Perpetual existence;*
e. *Status to prosecute and defend* legal action; and
f. Possible *favorable tax treatment.*

Unfortunately, too many new business owners rely on their *accountants* for advice on incorporating. This is a serious mistake, since most accountants are simply not trained to evaluate the legal aspects involved. Furthermore, a defectively incorporated entity will not protect its principals, nor offer the other advantages available. The advice of a competent *attorney* should be sought. The cost should not exceed $750 plus filing fees and state tax prepayment. If you attempt a do-it-yourself job, you may find yourself from midlife to retirement without a pension.

3. Licenses

Most states have over 100 different types of professional and vocational licenses or permits. The requirements for issuance vary widely, but usually include education, experience, passage of an examination, references, bonding, and other items designed to insure minimum standards of competence (and maximum government revenue). A local business license as well as health and safety permits may be required.

Federal licenses are mandated for numerous activities including investment advice; preparing meat; manufacturing alcohol, tobacco, drugs, or firearms; etc.

Contacting someone who is now in the field you wish to enter will save you a lot of time when you can least spare it (you'll be anxious to step up to the plate—a good sign). You can also call the state offices for licensing information. Then discuss your plans with your accountant and attorney.

4. Name

The name should project the image and describe the type of business. If you overlook these important marketing considerations, you are foreclosing business just because potential customers don't know what you do. Bev and Carole's business is Candyland, Inc. (they're the "Candyland," I'm the "Inc."). You can tell what they do, and the name conjures up an image of a whimsical world of lollipops and peppermint sticks. Their colors are red and white, and their logo looks like a picture on the cover of a fairy tale book. Below the logo are the words "The Home of Creative Candies." This is how to maximize your business identity.

5. Insurance

It is amazing how many new business owners over-insure. As with advertising, inventory, telephone systems, and other variable expenses, there is no limit to the amount you can spend.

If you incorporate, your personal liability is minimized immediately. Minimized, but not eliminated.

Property, casualty, life, health, and disability insurance are only a few of the items that are available. It's bewildering. The best advice I can give you is this: Call a reputable broker or agent. Tell him you will pay him $100 for an hour of his time to visit you and analyze what you absolutely need. State unequivocally that you *don't* intend to buy *anything*. An ethical one will honor this arrangement, and personally review the types of insurance available, making recommendations. You will not feel pressured to buy and will receive objective advice. It's not the $100, it's the respect for the professional time. That investment will probably save you thousands of dollars in premiums the first year alone.

Once you start hiring employees, workers' compensation, unemployment, social security, and other insurance will be mandatory. You'll also be considering group health and life insurance. Until then, older but bolder is the way to be.

6. Sales Taxes

Since it's "Candyland," not "Fantasyland," even the queen pays taxes. Most states require businesses that sell any kind of goods to collect a tax from the customer and send it to the state or local entity. A major exception is goods being shipped out of the state.

7. Income Taxes

Believe it or not, these are actually fun to pay on a business the first time! It is an indication that you are succeeding.

The income tax procedure at the state level generally follows the federal law. Quarterly estimated taxes are remitted, and the tax is based upon net income of an individual or partnership.

A corporation also pays the tax, based upon net income. Then the owner (usually an officer) receives salary as an employee. Because two sets of books are required (corporate and individual), accounting fees can be higher. However, as with legal fees, they are tax-deductible, and the corporate tax structure can be advantageous.

A *certified* public accountant is well worth the slightly

higher fee, since an audit may eventually occur. Ask for the recommendation of a good, inexpensive bookkeeper for routine items or purchase a "one-write system" and fight through the numbers yourself for a while.

There are other things, of course. However, you can see that there is really nothing that frightening about the legalities of owning your own business. You'll make your share of mistakes, as everyone does. You'll also learn from them just like that extremely successful client I told you about in Chapter 2.

According to official statistics, over one-third of all retail sales in America are through franchises, and the probability of success is much higher for a franchised business.[21] In representing franchisors *and* franchisees, the reasons for this have become apparent: Under optimum conditions, there is a common interest, common identity, unique product line, and assistance from the franchisor. The franchisee immediately becomes part of a team, with all of the communication, support, and competitiveness that keeps everyone motivated.

Unfortunately, the opposite can occur as well. The franchisee can join and obtain nothing but zany advice, no support, and restrictive covenants from shedding the franchise and continuing independently.

There are primarily two ways the franchisor is paid: An initial "franchise fee" (which can vary from nothing to hundreds of thousands of dollars), and a "royalty" on gross income or sales (which also varies widely).

While it is not my intention to discuss franchising except in passing, here is the checklist we developed for clients to help them determine whether they should purchase a franchise:

1. What *amount of capital* will be required?
2. What is the *franchise fee?*
3. What is the *royalty?*

4. What will be *offered* in the franchise package (site selection, operating manuals, training programs, etc.)?
5. Are some offices *company-owned?*
6. Will an *exclusive territory* be granted?
7. What are the *reporting requirements* to and from the franchisees?
8. How are the *costs of advertising* shared?
9. How are the franchisees *attracted, screened,* and *trained?*
10. What are the *controls upon the franchisor* regarding deviation from the concept, failure to perform, competition with the franchisees, etc.?

Since franchises depend upon conformity, uniformity, and paperwork for their survival, the most successful franchisees tend to be good administrators. Creative owner-managers sometimes find that they are prevented from making operational changes they perceive as advantageous.

There is a direct relationship between the cost to purchase and maintain a franchise, and the amount of risk involved. This is a business reality that can be easily forgotten in the optimism of starting a new business venture.

In *How to Select a Franchise,* the senior associate in our Newport Beach office, Erwin Keup, shares his quarter-century of experience in franchising law, advising:

> [N]ot every franchise is a sure-fire success to multiply your savings and provide you with an enjoyable occupation for your remaining days on this planet . . . The average American doesn't trust his government, his legislature, politicians or even his own children, but he will trust anyone who puts on a flashy exterior and promises him a quick buck. We listen to only what we want to hear. For some reason, we believe all con-men wear flashy suits and have slicked down hair.
> . . . Most people have the mistaken idea that a lot of

money can be made with a minimum amount of effort. This is a serious mistake. It always has been my experience that the franchisee that works the hardest makes the most.[22]

Although I have advised consulting with an attorney before establishing any business, nowhere is this more important than in the purchase of a franchise. State disclosure laws are woefully inadequate to protect a purchaser. Looking before you leap makes it less likely that you will find this out for yourself.

If you are interested in the most thorough survey of franchises available, ask the reference librarian for the current edition of the *Franchise Opportunities Handbook,* annually published by the United States Department of Commerce. It contains no-nonsense descriptions of hundreds of legitimate franchisors in outline form that facilitates comparison (length of time in business, number of franchisees, training and management provided, financial assistance available, etc.).

Finding, starting, and running a business is complicated, and no amount of research will give you all the answers. But if you've got the urge—*go for it!*

CHAPTER **13**

Where You've Been Is Nowhere Compared to Where You're Going!

In *Life Is Tremendous,* one of our most gifted American philosophers, Charles "Tremendous" Jones, analogizes life to a psychological key ring. When we are born, the ring is empty, and each experience adds another key. That's where you've been. What you *do* with the keys determines where you're going. Charlie calls it the "law of exposure to experience." Here is the midlife motivator himself:

> This is an exciting law, because its practice makes things get better and better with added years . . . Eventually you know which keys unlock the door, and you slip through while the inexperienced people search feverishly to see if they have the key. The old-timer who is learning the law of exposure to experience doesn't need the stamina that he once needed; he knows how to get to the heart of a problem and prescribe a remedy . . .

> Most people who are getting old waste time wishing they were young again. I don't wish I were young again . . . the young are miserable with unanswered questions . . .

> You have to take the main route through all the traffic, but it gets you where you want to go.[23]

Let's take a look at some case studies of midlifers who recently entered the job market or changed careers:

Name: Thomas H. Bonner
Age: 60
Occupation: Executive vice president of a small manufacturing company
Income: $68,000 per year
History: When I first met Tom Bonner he was 56 years old and mentally retired. He thought his job as general manager of the assembly plant of a multinational company was the end of the line. He was a "company man," with 21 years of service, fully vested in the pension plan, and responsible for over 2,000 employees.

Tom's job had no challenge. He worked his way up from a job as a production control expediter, and the plant was profitable. His job became relegated to a maximum of three productive hours per day, and the rest was spent reading business periodicals, playing with the practice golf set in his office, and drinking during increasingly long lunch hours. As with so many midlifers, Tom didn't realize how much he had stagnated. Like age, it just crept up on him. There he was, a walking midlife mummy. Then, one day, an executive recruiter client of ours called him. That was the first day of the rest of his midlife.

The recruiter had been retained by a small competitor of Tom's company to find someone with his experience. After a little help with preparing a midlife resume and a psychological facelift, he was ready to interview.

The advantages of a small company had never really occurred to Tom, since he was so entrenched in his job. However, he soon learned that his salary requirements were no problem, because unlike with a large employer:

1. There were no training programs;
2. No middle management existed to promote;

3. The company was growing;
4. The overhead expenses were far less; and
5. The employee benefits were limited.

This is often the case with smaller employers, making their corporate environment ideal for midlifers.

After a few interviews with members of the board of directors and officers of one small competitor, Tom became excited about the contribution he could make by utilizing his manufacturing background. His wife had long since realized that his middle-age spread and over-sleeping were caused by "executive burn-out," so she knew a job change was long overdue.

The new company realized that its growth was limited because top management lacked the depth of understanding necessary to expand in manufacturing-related areas. Tom was earning $50,000, and an offer of $59,000 with the title of Executive Vice President was made to him. Stock options and a company car closed the deal. That small competitor has doubled its sales in the two years since Tom joined it, as a direct result of his efforts.

When I asked Tom if he wanted to pass anything along to you, he replied:

> To stay youthful,
> stay useful!

The sparkle in his eyes and the spring in his step speak for themselves.

Name: Brenda L. Harrison
Age: 57
Occupation: Stockbroker
Income: $60,000 per year
History: In 36 years as an "Army wife" Brenda had followed her husband around the world more times than she

cared to remember. Her mission in life was to raise their three children. Then, 12 years ago, her husband was permanently stationed near a major university. Brenda pursued a bachelor of arts degree in Spanish literature, but it hardly prepared her for a career in the business world. Suddenly, her husband died, leaving her with expenses far above the military death benefits.

After a brief period of understandable shock, then panic, Brenda decided she would organize her life by finding a job that would make up for all those years behind an apron.

There were four requirements:

1. Financial reward commensurate with effort;
2. Working with people rather than things;
3. An entrepreneurial atmosphere without a corporate hierarchy; and
4. Training at the employer's expense.

Sales was the obvious choice. Brenda had enjoyed financial planning for her family, so narrowed the options to the banking, insurance, real estate, and securities fields. Securities was chosen.

Because she recognized that being a middle-age woman made her different from the young male-dominated world of account executives, she developed a success principle:

> Whatever makes you different,
> makes you better.

Almost immediately, she was hired and trained by a national securities broker. Now she leads her office in sales, enjoying every moment of her working midlife. Her breadth of experience, coupled with a knowledge of the securities market, have earned her the respect of the entire organization and many awards. Clients won't use anyone else.

Name: Edward O. Parker
Age: 53
Occupation: Indoor plant business owner
Income: $35,000 per year
History: Three years ago, if anyone had suggested to Ed Parker that he would soon leave his secure job of 15 years as chief accountant with an advertising agency, he would probably have dismissed the idea. Then, one day, he happened to be passing through the reception area, looking for his staff. There they were, buying houseplants from a young man. Since Ed raised houseplants as a hobby, he was intrigued. He invited the fellow into his office, and soon learned that he was an independent contractor who purchased the plants from a local greenhouse. Unfortunately, the man could not return them, so was unwilling to experiment with new types of plants or to expand his sales force. Selling on consignment was the obvious answer.

Ed's son was a carpenter and was hired by his father to build a greenhouse on the patio. His next job was more permanent, as a part-time caretaker for the plants.

Now, every morning from 7:30 to 8:30, a parade of salespeople march through the backyard of the Parker home and leave with houseplants. Ed is the last to go, on his way to the office.

The neighbors don't object to business being conducted in their residential area, since they receive free plants regularly. In fact, Ed has become somewhat of a local celebrity. He now writes a weekly column on houseplant maintenance for the local newspaper and is a member of the city beautification committee. He's even working on videotaping segments for use by an early-morning television show!

With almost no investment, Ed has developed an annuity for the rest of his life. If he left his regular job tomorrow, he would just expand his activities at home. Although he's tempted to do so now, he's still enjoying looking for his staff.

I asked Ed how he was able to find the time, and he replied, "Many middle-age people are already working a four-day week. It just takes them five days to do it!"

Name: Margaret C. Bentley
Age: 52
Occupation: Owner of a computer store
Income: $70,000 per year
History: Margaret was a teacher with a metropolitan school district for over 25 years when she was almost stabbed to death trying to break up a fight between two students. The month-long hospital stay gave her time to think about her future. She had always been single, and her career was her life. Unfortunately, teaching school had become nothing more than a dangerous babysitting job, and she was ready for a change. Her comment was, "I was aging, but not growing. Teaching the students was no longer fun . . . it became a matter of survival, financially and physically." Margaret was *definitely* ready for a change.

She had taught math and was fascinated by personal computers. A computer store had just opened in a local shopping mall, and her first excursion out of the house while recuperating was to its grand opening. She talked to the manager, but didn't have the nerve to ask for a job. Then, she remembered something her father told her when she was a child:

> There's no need for courage
> if you're not scared.

The next day she was back asking for a position. Did she get it? No. But she got courage.

On her way home, she stopped at the phone company business office and picked up the current Yellow Pages for the surrounding areas. Then she tore into them Consultant Phone Call style. She figured, "If I can teach those kids, I can sell anything." Within a week, she was on a minimum-wage draw against commissions in a personal computer store, learning the difference between a power switch and a keyboard. Soon, she was back teaching— about computers, to government agencies and public schools.

Today, five years later, Margaret owns a franchise with the same organization that she originally worked for, and operates one of the most successful stores in its chain. She teaches computer care and feeding in her own classroom at the store.

Name: Howard N. Talley
Age: 46
Occupation: Pet boarding business owner
Income: $45,000 per year
History: Howard was one of those midlifers who never outgrew his love for dogs. As a child he wanted to become a veterinarian, but the family business was a barber shop, so his career was a foregone conclusion. His wife worked as a secretary for a local cosmetics manufacturer, and hated every minute of it. Animals were her love too, but there was nobody to care for them during the day. They had no children.

His fortieth birthday was the turning point. The thought of spending his midlife as a haircutting robot led to a discussion that evening about the future. The result was a very tired but excited Howard when the barber shop opened the next morning: a pet boarding business was born.

During their discussions, the Talleys devoured the weekend newspaper and located several old farm houses about ten miles away. Eventually, they bought one of them and sold their home in the city.

Today, The Pet Hotel has four-legged, well-groomed guests of every shape and size. And two very happy mid-life hosts!

Name: Janet K. Loren
Age: 45
Occupation: Manager of quality assurance for a medium-sized division of a large manufacturing company
Income: $60,000 per year
History: Janet and I worked for the same electronics manufacturing company 14 years ago. She was a quality control inspector, and I remember how excited she was to attend our in-house management training course when she was promoted to "leadperson."

Janet received only average reviews as an inspector, but was considered a "natural" supervisor. She had the ability to communicate with employees from the president of the company to the people on the line. Our office processed her requests for educational reimbursement every semester as she pursued management and engineering courses leading to a bachelor's degree.

At the age of 35, Janet married for the second time. The following year she requested a maternity leave for the usual reason. Since midlife motherhood was particularly fulfilling to her, she decided to remain at home. During this time, she finished the last year of college on a full-time schedule, and graduated with a B.S.E.E. degree.

When she was ready to return to work six years ago, Janet called our former employer. Since the company was laying off in the manufacturing area, no openings existed. I showed her the midlife resume format contained in Chapter 6 and suggested that she contact a client of ours who specializes in engineering placement.

The recruiter was a franchisee of a national organization and, after placing Janet's background in its system, received a call from another office in the Midwest regarding an opening there for a manager of quality assurance with a medium-sized division of an international company.

Fortunately Janet's husband was an outside salesperson, so relocating was not a major problem. After two interviews, she re-entered the job market with a $14,000 increase above her former job, fully paid relocation expenses, and became the first woman in the history of the company to supervise a manufacturing department.

I didn't ask Janet for a quote—her favorite by Ralph Waldo Emerson is on her office wall:

> The years teach much
> which the days never know.

One of the great thrills of my midlife has been to see how people like this have grown.

Success in job hunting requires a candid, sometimes painful, look at ourselves. In the competitive economic world, we are just a commodity in the marketplace—only as good as our last project, our last sale, our last shipment. This is the law of business.

Ever since I was old enough to read, I have been studying the lives of successful people. The majority of them started with nothing and attained their success during midlife. What makes them so extraordinary? Opportunity helps, talent helps, but there is really only one crucial answer:

> People who are successful in midlife have the ability to draw on their experience and focus maximum energy in a disciplined way.

This is more than just an observation. These are the words above the portals to a happier, more productive midlife. For in them we find a formula that can be practically and systematically applied to tap the incredible potential within you, supercharge you along the way, and assure that you will never have to be at the mercy of any employer again.

It's simple, but it's not obvious. Just as the people we admire have that almost imperceptible "edge," "timing," "savvy"—that "sixth sense"—so it is with understanding how to use the keys themselves.

Fortunately, it won't take you volumes or years to get down to business. You just have to apply the principles in this book to your life. Gradually, but powerfully, they will become "habit knit" into your thinking process. Success in finding a job isn't an end at all—it's just another key.

As you have progressed through this book, I invited some of the greatest authorities the world has ever known to join us. This is because the personal and *personnel* effectiveness of the approach lies in its combination of techniques to help you to get *whatever* you want. A job? Sure. Happiness, money, power, friends. In fact, anything realistic that you can imagine.

Which will it be? A random, wandering, "just passin' through" existence, or a "go for it," exciting one-on-one adventure in the real give-and-take, up-and-down, reap-as-you-sow midlife job market?

You must have realized by now that you no longer need the old excuses: "I'm too old to . . . " "I'm too weak to . . . " "When I was younger, I could . . . " "I don't have the training to . . . " "It's just too hard for me to . . . " "What will my _____ think of me if I . . . " and so on.

The only way to overcome this negativism is by positive programming. If you find yourself procrastinating, make a *financial* commitment in some way—buy one of the books, subscribe to a trade magazine, or enroll in a training program. This helps to overcome the initial inertia against any change. The early stages of self-development are the most fragile.

During a recent tour, I found myself in front of a microphone on an all-night radio talk show somewhere west of New York. I ran out of fingers counting the number of interviews that day, and was due to catch a plane to the next city. Since they're so much easier to catch when they're on the ground, the host announced that the next call would be the last. The caller asked, "What does the 'J.D., C.P.C.' after your name mean?" Of course, the straight answer would be have been, "Juris Doctor and Certified Placement Counselor." But I just couldn't be straight under the circumstances. As I removed the headset and stood up to leave, my candid reply said it all: "The 'J.D.' stands for 'Just Do It!,' and the 'C.P.C.' stands for 'Courage, Persistence, and Confidence!' "

You're only young once, but you're only older once too. Start a steamroller that will move mountains . . . *your* mountains.

HAVE A GREAT MIDLIFE!

Bibliography . . . and Why

In the "Welcome Address" of *Og Mandino's University of Success,* the Dean of Admissions states:

> Undoubtedly those years you spent in school taught you many things. But during all those hours spent in all those classes, *never,* not even for a single 50-minute period, were you taught or shown how to apply what you were learning in order to achieve a life filled with happiness, accomplishment and success.[24]

That is the reason I have integrated quotes from books that can help you to succeed quickly during midlife and can also give you the depth of understanding that you'll need to improve the rest of your life. They can all be obtained readily, and are available in paperback.

Self-help books are to the midlife mind what vitamins are to the midlife body: They all look alike and the ingredients might be similar, but it's the *way they are formulated* that makes the difference. You automatically assimilate what you need and discard the rest. Try to take too many vitamins too fast, and you'll end up with an upset stomach. With self-help books, you'll become confused and discouraged.

But most important, vitamins don't work on an empty stomach. Self-help books don't work in a vacuum either. That's why readers of motivational books frequently complain, "I didn't learn anything new . . . I want something I can *use!*" Therefore, I tied the most powerful ones to practical books on jobseeking, and wrapped them together in one systematic, step-by-step approach. It's really very scientific.

If you read the books in the order they are presented, you'll be maximizing their effectiveness.

It is no coincidence that this section began with *Og Mandino's University of Success*. It is an extraordinary book, containing excerpts from 50 works by the greatest authorities on human nature of the twentieth century. With his usual brilliance, Og introduces each "lesson" and gives the reasons for its inclusion. This is an outstanding achievement, and is the closest you will find to a complete midlife success reference library in one mighty paperback.

How to Win Friends and Influence People by Dale Carnegie is the all-time bestseller of the century for people in midlife. Although the Carnegie name is sometimes associated with an overly-aggressive sales personality, this is probably because some of the courses are in that field. Read the book once, and you'll go back to it again and again. Fifteen million copies, 2.5 million students, classes in 57 countries around the world. That's *really* middle-age spread! And that's the reason I used the book for the "smile technique." It sounds so obvious, but it's so subtle that I wanted you to accept it without hesitation.

Now that we've gone through your basic training, it's time to march out onto the battlefield. Let's roll out the heavy artillery:

Closing on Objections by Paul Hawkinson is a midlifer's mortar. Unlike books commercially available, the cover proclaims that it is "Exclusively for the Placement and Recruiting Professional." Since it contains tricks of the trade in getting people hired, it could formerly be ordered only by prescription (a request on placement service letterhead). It was also printed on paper that self-destructed if photocopied. However, it is such a valuable resource that I have arranged with the publisher for a slightly expurgated version to be printed for midlife applicants. Write to Research Information Bureau at the address in the Bibliography for ordering information.

Then, *How to Turn an Interview into a Job*. Jeff Allen for jobseekers of all ages. I thank you. You'll thank you.

I can't drop down too far without mentioning *Looking Out for Number One*. Although I've been accused of being Robert Ringer's ghostwriter, I'm not. It's just that we look at life the same way. If you've let the years go by without reading it, you're in for a treat. I don't know of another book that takes as much humor, wisdom, and truth from the middle years, and formulates a better plan of attack on an unsuspecting world. It can change your life.

Michael Korda's *Success!* presents profiles of many midlifers who have paid their dues wisely. It also gives practical advice on adapting success principles to enhance your career. It is a business-oriented book that can be read again and again. Each time you sharpen your competitive edge.

Books on negotiating are valuable only if you can apply the techniques. As a student of this subject, I find that the pressures of the negotiating process often tend to structure the dialogue. One of the reasons the techniques work so well in lawyering and jobseeking is that the reactions and environment are so predictable, making the victim so controllable. We have discussed all you need to know already, but two completely different books are useful to help you enhance other areas of your midlife. Initially, *You Can Negotiate Anything* by Herb Cohen. Although you might think Herb is missing a few midlife marbles, it is funny and fast reading. *Winning by Negotiation* by Tessa Albert Warschaw is the runner-up. Tessa's warm, sensitive style, and concern with the special problems of midlife women are the reasons for honorable mention.

The credible books on body language, "kinesthetics," "nonverbal communication," and other pseudosciences all caution that the same dance may be the result of different music. However, since all people who are hiring have similar pressures, their physical telegraphy can be easily discerned and used to psych them out. That's why pacing and leading (as discussed in Chapter 8) is the clincher when you're in the operating room. One of the first books on the subject was *How to Read a Person Like a Book* by Gerard Nierenberg and Henry Calero. It is still the best primer on the subject by two senior negotiators.

So many books in the career field are either too abstract or just too shallow to be turning any midlives around. For this reason, I am pleased to recommend two new ones that are direct and thorough in the areas of job sharing and temporary assignments: *The Complete Guide to Job Sharing* by Patricia Lee and *Working Whenever You Want* by Barbara Johnson. If either alternative appeals to you, these books will teach you all you need to know.

Two of the finest books for networking lists are *The National Job Finding Guide* by Heinz Ulrich and Robert Connor, and *The Encyclopedia of Associations* by Denise Akey. Although the former hasn't been updated since 1981, most of the contact information is still correct. As I mentioned when we discussed networking, these paperbacks are also found on most library reference shelves. Libraries are long on lists, so plan to spend some time. Since you don't need most of the information, the library photocopy machine is your best investment.

If you are suffering from midlife "axe anxiety," and need help staying on the job long enough to leave on your own terms, *Office Politics* by Marilyn Moats Kennedy is for you. In addition to providing usable jobkeeping hints, it stresses the importance of networking. This is because the most you can usually hope for is just hangin' in there a little longer. *Super Threats* was selected because its authors, John Striker and Andrew Shapiro, show you how to position yourself properly if you must start mentioning the equal employment opportunity and wrongful termination laws.

Entrepreneur Magazine is the newsstand publication of the American Entrepreneurs Association. Each month, stories about successful small businesses and indispensable ideas for their operation are presented. The AEA also offers over 250 start-up business manuals ranging from "Antique Shops" to "Sailboat Time-Share Leasing," at under $50 each. Its building in Los Angeles is a virtual fountain of innovative short-cutting ideas for new business ventures. The address of the AEA is in the Bibliography.

How to Select a Franchise takes all of the fancy words and hype out of this misused and misunderstood concept, and guides the investor toward an intelligent decision. As I mentioned, Erwin Keup is an associate of ours, so I have seen the value of his approach. We meet so many midlifers who have slaved and saved only to lose it all to some knave. If you think franchising is for you, I recommend the book highly. Use it with the *Franchise Opportunities Handbook* published by the United States Department of Commerce, and you're in business (well, almost).

Life Is Tremendous is Charles "Tremendous" Jones's ammunition for the battle of the bulge. It is largely philosophical but contains the wisdom of someone who obeys the law of exposure to experience.

There are thousands of biographies about successful midlifers available in bookstores and libraries. As you read, you will start to identify with them. One book a month is the recommended dosage. The best general "collected biography" for midlifers is *American Dreams: Lost and Found* by Studs Terkel.

Integrate the techniques you have learned into your midlife, and read these books with the idea of deepening your understanding. If you do, midlife jobseeking will be the blueprint for a life of success, happiness, and peace of mind.

BIBLIOGRAPHY

Akey, Denise S., *The Encyclopedia of Associations,* Detroit, Michigan, Gale Research Co., 1984.

Allen, Jeffrey G., J.D., C.P.C., *How to Turn an Interview into a Job,* New York, New York, Simon & Schuster, 1983.

American Entrepreneurs Association, 2311 Pontius Avenue, Los Angeles, California 90064.

Carnegie, Dale, *How to Win Friends and Influence People,* New York, New York, Pocket Books, 1981.

Cohen, Herb, *You Can Negotiate Anything,* New York, New York, Bantam Books, 1980.

Dictionary of Occupational Titles, Washington, D.C., United States Department of Labor, 1984.

Franchise Opportunities Handbook, Washington, D.C., United States Department of Commerce, 1984.

Hawkinson, Paul A., *Closing on Objections,* Research Information Bureau, Post Office Box 9653, Kirkwood, Missouri 63122.

Johnson, Barbara L., *Working Whenever You Want,* Englewood Cliffs, New Jersey, Prentice-Hall, Inc., 1983.

Jones, Charles T., *Life Is Tremendous,* Harrisburg, Pennsylvania, Executive Books, 1968.

Kennedy, Marilyn Moats, *Office Politics,* New York, New York, Warner Books, 1981.

Keup, Erwin J., *How to Select a Franchise,* Newport Beach, California, Consigliare Publications, 1982.

Korda, Michael, *Success!,* New York, New York, Ballantine Books, 1978.

Lee, Patricia, *The Complete Guide to Job Sharing,* New York, New York, Walker & Co., 1983.

Mandino, Og, *Og Mandino's University of Success,* New York, New York, Bantam Books, 1982.

Nierenberg, Gerard I., and Henry H. Calero, *How to Read a Person Like a Book,* New York, New York, Cornerstone Library, 1972.

Ringer, Robert J., *Looking Out for Number One,* New York, New York, Fawcett Crest Books, 1978.

Striker, John M., and Andrew O. Shapiro, *Super Threats*, New York, New York, Dell Publishing Co., 1978.

Terkel, Studs, *American Dreams: Lost and Found*, New York, New York, Ballantine Books, 1981.

Ulrich, Heinz, and J. Robert Connor, *The National Job Finding Guide*, Garden City, New York, Doubleday & Co., 1981.

Warschaw, Tessa Albert, *Winning by Negotiation*, New York, New York, Berkley Publishing Corp., 1981.

Footnotes

1. *Statistical Abstract of the United States* by the United States Bureau of the Census, 1982.
2. Age Discrimination in Employment Act of 1967, 29 USC 621 et seq.
3. Vocational Rehabilitation Act of 1974, 29 USC 701 et seq.
4. Vocational Rehabilitation Act of 1974, 29 USC 701 et seq.
5. Equal Pay Act of 1963, 29 USC 206 et seq.; Title VII of the Civil Rights Act of 1964, as amended by the Equal Employment Opportunity Act of 1972, 42 USC 2000e et seq.
6. *Looking Out for Number One* by Robert J. Ringer.
7. *How to Win Friends and Influence People* by Dale Carnegie.
8. *Super Threats* by John M. Striker and Andrew O. Shapiro.
9. "In Camera: Hon. Frank K. Richardson," *California Lawyer*, May 1984.
10. *You Can Negotiate Anything* by Herb Cohen.
11. "In Camera: Hon. Frank K. Richardson," *California Lawyer*, May 1984.
12. *How to Read a Person Like a Book* by Gerard I. Nierenberg and Henry H. Calero.
13. *How to Turn an Interview into a Job* by Jeffrey G. Allen, J.D., C.P.C.
14. *Closing on Objections* by Paul A. Hawkinson.
15. *Closing on Objections* by Paul A. Hawkinson.
16. *Office Politics* by Marilyn Moats Kennedy.
17. *Winning by Negotiation* by Tessa Albert Warschaw.
18. *Winning by Negotiation* by Tessa Albert Warschaw.
19. *Success!* by Michael Korda.
20. "A Word from the Publisher," *Entrepreneur Magazine*, March 1984.

21. *Franchise Opportunities Handbook* by United States Department of Commerce, 1984.

22. *How to Select a Franchise* by Erwin J. Keup.

23. *Life Is Tremendous* by Charles T. Jones.

24. *Og Mandino's University of Success* by Og Mandino.

Index

About the Authors

Jeffrey G. Allen, J.D., C.P.C., is America's leading placement attorney. His combined experience as a certified placement counselor, personnel manager, and professional negotiator uniquely qualify him as an authority on the hiring process. Mr. Allen was appointed Special Advisor to the American Employment Association and is General Counsel to the California Association of Personnel Consultants. He writes a nationally syndicated column entitled "Placements and The Law," conducts seminars, and is regularly featured in television, radio, and newspaper interviews. He is author of the bestseller *How to Turn an Interview into a Job,* also published by Simon and Schuster.

Jess Gorkin was for thirty years editor-in-chief of *Parade* magazine, and more recently spent five years as editor of *50 Plus* magazine. In the course of a long and distinguished career as writer and editor he received two citations for magazine reporting from the Overseas Press Club and three Fourth Estate Awards, among many others. At his death in 1985 he was active as a consulting editor of *Parade.*